English for Business

Second edition

W Ferrier Mavor MA, FRSA

PITMAN
150
YEARS

PITMAN PUBLISHING
128 Long Acre London WC2E 9AN

© W Ferrier Mavor 1980

First published in Great Britain 1971
Second edition 1980
Reprinted 1986, 1987

Text set in 10/12 pt VIP Plantin
Printed and bound in Great Britain by
Richard Clay Ltd, Bungay, Suffolk

ISBN 0 273 01428 5

Contents

Acknowledgments

The author and publishers have made every effort to trace the copyright holders of material used in the book and wish to thank the following for permission to reprint the material indicated:

Churchill, Sir W S, *My Early Life*, Fontana, 1972, p 2

Quiller-Couch, Sir A, *On the Art of Writing*, Cambridge, v

Thackeray, W M, *Vanity Fair*, Everyman Publishers, 1963, p 2

'All weather sports pitches', *World Peace Magazine*, Nigeria, 1978, p 159

'Another feather in SSE's cap', *The Straits Times*, Singapore, 1979, pp 161–2

'Business as usual', *Spectator*, 1970, pp 163–4

'Learning at a distance', *Open University Handbook*, 1979, p 157

'Partnership in the office', *You and Your Secretary*, The Industrial Society, 1977, pp 167–8

'Prospects bleak for business graduates', *The Straits Times*, Singapore, 1979, pp 166–7

'Shop talk', *School Leaver*, Dominion Press, 1977, pp 160–1

'The Tycoon's World', *Spectator*, 1970, pp 164–5

'Training for today's jobs', *Office Skills*, Pitman, 1978, pp 169–70

London Chamber of Commerce for the exam papers on pp 127–8, 136, 175, 178–9

Northern Counties Technical Exam Council for the exam paper on pp 137–8

Preface

This revised edition of *English for Business* is both a textbook and a reference book with these aims—to help students in Britain and overseas towards a more concise, lucid and correct expression of English; to provide model forms of business communication; to supply a wide range of exercises for practice; to stimulate interest in words and their function; but most important of all, to illustrate the force of simple and direct English. It also aims to provide revision practice for the older person seeking to break into the office field.

Each of us writes to be understood; this is the first principle of any writing. So there can be no more appropriate introduction than these words of Sir Arthur Quiller-Couch:

> Let me remind you that you cannot use the briefest, the humblest process of thought, cannot so much as resolve to take your bath hot or cold, or decide what to order for breakfast, without forecasting it to yourself in some form of words. Words are, in fine, the only currency in which we can exchange thought even with ourselves. Does it not follow then, that the more accurately we use words the closer definition we shall give to our thoughts? Does it not follow that by drilling ourselves to write perspicuously we train our minds to clarify their thought?

FM 1980

1 The long and the short sentence

Our aim in all writing should be to avoid monotony. This is not always easy. Essentially, we have to be interested in what we are writing. This is more than half the battle towards clear and competent expression. Should we use long or short sentences or a mixture of both? It would be unwise to lay down any rigid rules for the use of the short and the long sentence, but these guidelines should help:

Short sentences are used:

a to express rapidity of event, movement, or tense situations
b to drive home points or to sum up an argument
c in definitions

Long sentences are used:

a in descriptive passages
b to develop a reasoned argument
c to build up background
d to give weight and dignity to the writing

Here are some examples:

Jones saw his opportunity. The Chairman had finished speaking. The men seemed undecided. Jones pushed back his chair and got to his feet. He looked down at the factory floor. All the men waited for him to speak.

Notice how the tension has been built up by the use of short incisive sentences. Now look at the same sequence of events described much less dramatically.

As the Chairman finished speaking to the men, Jones, while they hesitated, saw his opportunity. He pushed back his chair and, getting to his feet, looked down at the factory floor where the men stood waiting for him to speak.

In this passage two sentences are used in place of the six of the first passage. A measured composition of words replaces the dramatics of the short sentences. So there is a choice, as there is in all writing, of selecting the method and means of writing.

A look at the punctuation of the two passages further illustrates their difference. The first passage contains no commas; the second has five. Read the second passage again to see how the comma pauses help the measured effect.

Here are three further passages.

1 When first in the dim light of early morning I saw the shores of Cuba rise and define themselves from dark-blue horizons, I felt as if I sailed with Long John Silver and first gazed on Treasure Island. Here was a place where real things were going on. Here was a scene of vital action. Here was a place where anything might happen. Here was a place where something would certainly happen. Here I might leave my bones. These musings were dispersed by the advance of breakfast, and lost in the hurry of disembarkation. (Extract from *My Early Life*, Churchill)

This is a superb example of the use of the short sentence to promote interest and tension. Note the stirring effect of the word 'here' at the beginning of the five short sentences. Notice also how the absence of commas helps to stimulate interest.

2 It may be remarked in the course of this little conversation (which took place as the coach rolled along lazily by the river-side) that, though Miss Rebecca Sharp has twice had occasion to thank Heaven, it has been, in the first place, for ridding her of some person whom she hated, and, secondly, for enabling her to bring her enemies to some sort of perplexity or confusion, neither of which is a very amiable motive for religious gratitude, or such as would be put forward by persons of a kind and placable disposition. (Extract from *Vanity Fair*, Thackeray)

Study the measured build-up of this single long sentence. Note how the commas, generously used, help this effect. Such effect is further emphasised by the two introductory words or phrases—'in the first place' and 'secondly'—which Thackeray uses to fulfil the word 'twice'. All in all, this is an orderly and compact long sentence.

3 My colleagues and I are thinking of the future role of your company. This role is that of an investment trust. It is our duty to earn dividends for our stockholders, but the function of the trust

should extend beyond that of merely collecting dividends. We feel this strongly. We should ensure that the funds at our disposal are used to the best advantage. This should be in the interests of industry in this country and in development overseas under private enterprise. In the overseas sphere our company has a big contribution to make.

Study this mixture of both the long and the short sentence. The first two short sentences help to emphasise what is to come—i.e. 'our duty'—and the final short sentence points the way ahead. The two long sentences help to balance the Chairman's statement.

In these three passages monotony of expression has been avoided and clarity of meaning has been achieved.

Long and short sentences, however, must be considered mainly in the context of business letters. Too many business letters contain sentences that are much too long. Look at this one:

We can provide two qualities of carpeting, namely Special grade suitable for bedrooms, if the intention is to provide luxury with endurance, and Plus grade for corridors and staircases where primary importance is long wear, both of which are available in a wide range of self-colours and patterns, with a three year guarantee against fading.

This sentence is ridiculously long—56 words; because of this it is a bad sentence. There is no crispness; it lacks clarity. It needs to be read several times before it can be fully understood. It is the type of sentence that should be banished from any business letter. Now look at a shortened version:

We stock two grades of carpeting suitable for your purpose. Our Special grade combines luxury with durability, recommended for bedrooms. Our Plus grade is long wearing, of good quality, suitable for corridors and staircases. Both grades are available in a wide range of self-colours and patterns. Both carry a three year guarantee against fading.

These short sentences—of 10, 10, 14, 13 and 8 words—are all crisp, clear and concise. This is the type of sentence, relevant and informative, that should be part of a business letter.

What, after all, is a long sentence? This is difficult to define, for there can be no inflexible rule about this. Perhaps the number of words in a sentence should be some kind of guide? If so, then try to keep your sentences to under 20 words and never exceed 30.

Remember that long sentences are bad for business letters. This is because long sentences are harder to understand; they tend to encourage inaccuracies of meaning and agreement; they invite wasted words.

What, then, are the advantages of short sentences? They promote clarity of meaning—and this is essential in the writing of business letters—they are much more positive than long sentences, and they help you to think logically.

Cultivate the short sentence. Do this by keeping sentences to under 20 words. These guidelines should help:

a include only the necessary ideas and relevant information
b let one sentence carry one idea, certainly never more than two
c omit all needless words
d use short words and commonplace words; shun abstract words
e when possible, be informal in style

Look at this final example of the short sentence:

Jones had a staff problem (5). He was not sure how to cope with it (9). He had thought about it for a long time (9). Suddenly, he felt that the answer might be some form of compromise (12). When he thought of it in this light, it became less of a problem (14). The answer, in fact, lay in compromise (7).

There is no waste of words. The words used are simple everyday ones. No sentence is longer than 14 words. The sentences follow each other in logical development, each carrying one thought or idea.

This, then, is what we have to strive for—economy of words, but with full meaning.

Exercise

1   Re-write these sentences in two long sentences:

A crate of ornaments was delivered this morning by your van. It appears to be the fulfilment of our order sent last week. Not all the items on our list have been sent. Three of the Worcester figures were broken. We are returning these. We are also sending a list of those not sent. We shall be glad to have the latter and replacement of the breakages forwarded as soon as possible.

2 In the long sentence below there are four main ideas. List these ideas and re-write the sentence in four short sentences.

When Mr Simpson was appointed we had hopes of promoting him to a managership in our organisation within perhaps two or three years, but his lack of initiative and grasp of responsibility have disappointed the Board of Directors, and because our firm's prospects have not advanced as we had hoped, we feel that there is little chance of promotion for Mr Simpson, at least until his work performance improves, coupled with the expansion of our organisation.

3 Which of these three sentences is the best for a business letter? Note that all contain the same essential information. Give reasons for your choice.

  a On receipt of your letter about the delay in delivery of your order we have looked into the matter and find that the delay was the result of the order being wrongly addressed.
  b Delivery of your order was delayed because it was wrongly addressed.
  c We have to inform you that delivery of your order was delayed because it was wrongly addressed.

2 Why we punctuate

The dictionary explains to punctuate as follows: to separate into sentences, clauses, etc., by periods, commas, colons, etc.; to emphasise in some significant manner; to interrupt at intervals. **Punctuation**, therefore, is the art or system of separating written words by the use of punctuation marks—the period, comma, colon, semicolon, etc.

More simply, what is punctuation and why is it used? It is the use of stops or breaks to indicate pauses and points in the flow of writing so that meaning may be clearly understood. Its basic purpose is to clarify the written word and, because of this, some argue that it is more important than spelling.

Punctuation is an essential part of writing. Without it even the best writing would be unintelligible. It is not a necessary evil, but rather a positive aid to the clarity of language and, as such, should be both a pleasure and a satisfaction. Why not make it so?

It is difficult to lay down rules of punctuation, for punctuation is partly a matter of taste. This is what William Cobbett, in his *English Grammar* of 1818, had to say about it:

> No two writers use the same punctuation; they never will. It is quite impossible to give any precise rules for its use. Much must be left to taste: something must depend upon the weight which we may wish to give to particular words or phrases; and something on the seriousness or the levity of the subject on which we are writing.

This is still true today. Punctuation is nearly as much a matter of the author's style as his choice of words. Yet, in considering both its aims and its uses, two main principles should be followed:

1 Punctuation should be based on the framework of the written word, not on the need to pause for breath.
2 Provided it does not cloud the meaning, the fewer stops or breaks used, the better.

At the same time try to understand the various marks of punctuation—and use them. For if you limit their use you handicap your style.

There are two types of punctuation. The more important is that of the stops or breaks in the written word. Of secondary importance—but none the less an essential part of punctuation—is the use of accessories. Look, then, at the chief points of punctuation.

Full stop or period

This is used:

a to indicate the end of a statement
- Thank you for your letter of 5 February. Yes. No.

There are two exceptions to this rule. The full stop is left out after the signature at the end of a letter and at the end of an address.

b after initials or abbreviations—this is partly a matter of personal taste
- H. Y. Patel, Col. Davidson, Rev. Hopkins, cum div., ad val., 11.30 a.m.

c in time, to separate hours and minutes—this is also a matter of personal taste
- Flight OP68 from Singapore is due to arrive at 17.50 hrs.

d to signify that words have been omitted. Normally there are three dots if the omission is in the middle of a sentence and four when the omission occurs after a completed sentence

Note that a full stop is not necessary:

a when the abbreviation ends with the last two letters of the word shortened
- 1st, 13th, 8vo (octavo), 4to (quarto)

b after words or figures used in tabular work (except decimal points)

c when the abbreviation begins and ends in the same letters as the original word
- Dr for doctor, Mr for mister, flt for flight, rd for road, st for street

d at the end of a heading
- Report, Memorandum, Agenda, Matters Arising, Notice of Assessment

e after titles of books, chapters, notices, songs, and the like
- The Concise Oxford Dictionary, Chapter Eight, Private Property, Hallelujah

Comma

After the full stop, the most important mark of punctuation is the comma. It is also the most flexible, the least bound by rules. It represents the shortest marked pause in a sentence, as opposed to the period which is the longest. Here are listed some of the main uses of the comma, with examples, and (where necessary) explanations.

1 It separates words or phrases forming a list or series, as in:
  ● The Chairman called attention to the fact that the expense items under wages, repairs, and taxes all showed a substantial increase.
  ● He was an efficient, conscientious, enthusiastic worker.
  ● The suitcase contained some old clothes, four paperback novels, a canvas bag of loose money, and a few bits of jewellery.
     Some argue that the comma should not be used before 'and' in a list. Others, and the author is one, believe that the comma used before 'and' often avoids ambiguity. For example, 'black, white, and green' refers to three objects each of a single different colour, but 'black, white and green, and red' refers to three objects one of which is in two colours, white and green.
     In the separation of phrases and short sentences joined by 'and' the comma is very often superfluous, but it is still used. Look at these examples:
  ● Restaurant prices were high, and the food was poor.
  ● He looked at himself in the mirror, and did not like what he saw.
     In neither of these two sentences is there any pause or emphasis that justifies a comma so it should be discarded. Take this example:
  ● He waited until the meeting was quiet, and then began his speech.
     Here the comma is justified by the pause after quiet. It adds emphasis to the sentence.

2 It separates introductory words or phrases from the rest of the sentence, for example:
  ● To sum up, I think we should consider three main issues.
  ● Fortunately, we were able to get seats on the next plane.

3 It separates words or phrases that have been written into the sentence without affecting the meaning of it.
  ● He will not, therefore, be available.
  ● There is, I should imagine, a reason for his absence.
     The above commas are, in fact, parenthetical. They act as brackets and when used like this they must always be in pairs.

4 It separates words or phrases which explain or expand the main idea.

- Dr Choo Sing, the delegate from Malaysia, spoke to the motion.
- The Works Manager, Mr Grady, held a very different view.

Note, however, that in one kind of apposition the comma is omitted. For example:

- My sister Susan lives in Yorkshire.

This implies that I have only one sister. But if I write: My sister, Susan, lives in Yorkshire—the implication is, because of the commas, that I have more than one sister.

5 It separates an absolute or complete phrase from the rest of the sentence.

- The chairman having arrived, the meeting quickly got under way.
- As this is your view, I have to disagree with you.

6 It separates figures in large numbers into groups of hundreds.
- 68,034   769,000   9,000,000

This use of the comma is fast disappearing.

7 It introduces speech.

- She asked, 'What is the price of these apples?'
- He said, 'Please bring me the file on minor repairs, Anne.'

Look at the following examples and consider the use of commas or the absence of them.

1 The estimates quoted, as explained in our letter, stipulate payment within one month.

2 When the manager looked at the invoice he realised at once how the mistake had risen.

3 To err is human; to forgive, divine.

4 Can you deliver the lawn-mower tomorrow or Thursday?

5 Can you deliver the lawn-mower tomorrow, or Thursday?

6 O P Mitchell, Esq., BA.

7 As soon as he had telephoned he went out.

8 Immediately you telephoned, she came to see me.

The examples given above are all correct. Check why. Note particularly **4** and **5**.

Remember that of all punctuation points the comma is the least bound by rules. It can be a great aid to the understanding of a message. Use it, but guard against over-usage; rather use it sparingly.

Semicolon

This is much stronger than a comma; it has almost the strength of a full stop. It is used to separate statements which are closely connected in thought but are not linked grammatically, for example:

- The committee held the view that the matter should receive further consideration; they recommended that the secretary should make further inquiries and report at the next meeting.
- A good secretary, apart from knowing her secretarial skills, must be at ease when meeting people; she must have initiative and enthusiasm for her work; above all, she must be loyal to her employer and to her firm.

Now study these varied examples and consider how the semicolons have been used in each.

- His desk was covered with documents; in one tray catalogues spilled over; another was filled with a pile of books; pencils and pens stood stuck in a jar; there seemed to be little order anywhere.

Here the semicolons have been used firstly to separate phrases or items all closely connected, and secondly to introduce emphasis.

- The following have been invited: Mr & Mrs Mossman; Professor Peter Markham; Mr & Mrs Bruce Marshall; Sir James and Lady Cator; Miss Joan Gower; Ms Elizabeth Watson.

Semicolons here are preferable to commas, since commas would not be strong enough to separate these word groups.

- These letters are to the point; the others are quite irrelevant.

The semicolon balances the contrasting statements.

- She was a good trainee; she was conscientious; she had initiative; and, in due course, she passed her examination.

Here the semicolon has an accumulative or step-by-step effect.

These examples show how helpful the semicolon can be in the meaning and force of expression. Like the comma, however, it can be over-used.

Colon

The colon is not often used in continuous writing. Normally it introduces a series or catalogue of items, for example:

- The items discussed were: time and place of the next meeting, remuneration of agents, allocation of areas to each representative.
- The selection committee were looking for the following attributes: a knowledge of profit and loss accounts, the ability to handle a crisis, administrative initiative, progressive ideas.

The series or lists shown on page 10 often follow such sign-words as: the following, as follows, namely, for example.

The colon has other uses. Perhaps the most common is to introduce a quotation or direct speech, as in:

● The President began his address: 'My Lords, Ladies and Gentlemen.'

● The Chairman quoted from the Annual Report: 'The development in our markets abroad over the past year has exceeded our expectations.'

The following are examples of the explanatory colon and the balancing colon. The explanatory colon is perhaps the more common and the more useful, for example:

● He agreed: he had to: after all, it was his idea.

● I have a proposal to make: it is a reasonable one: here it is.

In both cases the pause effect demands a colon.

The balancing colon is used as follows:

● Jones is well able to carry the responsibility: and he will.

● No man with his wisdom could have done more: no man with his wisdom should have done less.

It could be argued that the above examples could have been written as short sentences. This is so, but in sentence form they would have been much less effective.

The colon is a difficult mark of punctuation, but one well worth understanding—and using.

Dash

The dash marks a parenthesis, for example:

● A week later—at the end of September—she handed in her resignation.

It is sometimes used to introduce an interpolation or insertion, as in:

● He asked me—despite the fact that I was a complete stranger to him—to support his nomination.

In both of these examples the words between the dashes represent a **parenthesis**—an insertion which is not grammatically essential to the sentence. When this is the case, the inserted words must be separated by two dashes. Here, the two dashes have almost the effect of brackets, e.g.

● A week later (at the end of September) she handed in her resignation.

Note, however, that the use of the double dash is more abrupt, more forceful than brackets.

The **single dash** is used:

a to sum up or gather a scattered subject
- Bells, whistles, sirens, hooters—all welcomed the yacht as she entered the harbour.

b to show, in writing, hesitation of speech
- The chairman was slow to find words. 'In the circumstances,' he began, 'I—er—would rather not commit the company—on this matter.'

c to show a sudden change of thought
- It had to be Jones—or maybe his assistant.

Exclamation mark

As the name implies, this is used after exclamatory words or emphatic comment, phrases or sentences, indicating surprise, shock, impatience.
- Alas! Hello! Heavens! Look what you've done! A fine friend you are! Hurrah! Hurry up!

Be careful not to use the exclamation mark merely to emphasise a statement, for example:
- It was a magnificent performance!

Here, there should be no exclamation mark.

Hyphen

This joins two or more words which are looked upon as one, e.g. rag-and-bone man. Often this joining becomes permanent, as in to-day and to-morrow, now written as one: today and tomorrow. Note-book is now notebook, just as bookcase is no longer book-case. There are many more examples of this disappearance of the hyphen.

The hyphen is also used to indicate that two vowels are to be pronounced separately:
- co-opt; co-ordinate; pre-empt; re-echo.

The most common use of the hyphen is to split into syllables a word broken up because of lack of space. When this happens the hyphen should be introduced early in the word, e.g. dis-enchanted, not disenchant-ed; or in the middle, e.g. inter-woven.

Always avoid cutting off the suffix *-ed*. If in doubt about where to put the hyphen, use the Concise Oxford Dictionary as your guide.

Apostrophe

This mark of punctuation can be a little confusing. It indicates the possessive case, as in: Jane's handbag; a month's holiday; a lifetime's work; Brown and Poulson's shops. These mean quite simply: the handbag of Jane; a holiday of a month; the work of a lifetime; the shops of Brown and Poulson. Its other uses in the singular are:

a to signify the omission of a letter or letters
  • There's no point in hurrying; we can't get home in time now.
b to indicate the plural of letters
  • There are two m's in accommodation.
  Note, however, that the apostrophe is *not* used in plurals such as: MPs, Phds, NCOs, etc.
c in names
  • O'Grady; O'Connor

It is the possessive plural that sometimes causes difficulty. Here are guides to its use:

a when the plural ends in s the apostrophe is added, as in:
  • the girls' dolls; five days' work
b when the plural does not end in s the apostrophe comes before the s:
  • women's rights; children's meals

Note the following, however:
  • St James's Square; H G Wells's books; Rees's car (singular); the Reeses' car (plural)

Lastly, we come to the 'accessories' to punctuation. There are three important ones: capitals, italics, and quotation marks.

Capitals

The use of capitals is much more a matter of taste than of rules, and because of this, opinion varies about when and where they should be used. The suggested guidelines attempt to be both logical and unambiguous. Capitals, then, are used:

1 For titles of persons, offices, countries, organisations and institutions, buildings, ranks, etc.—whether singular or plural, e.g.
  • the Duke of Edinburgh; Marshals of the Royal Air Force; the Inland Revenue; Malaysia; the Royal Society of Arts; the Foreign

Secretary; the Deputy Public Prosecutor; St Pancras Station; the Caribbean; the Archbishop of Canterbury; the Egyptian Ambassador.

2 When names are repeated in shortened form, it is normal to retain the capital for the shortened title, as shown in these examples:

● The Royal Society of Arts is for the development of the arts, manufactures, science and commerce. The Society is one of the oldest institutions of its kind in this country.

● Dr Srivasta wrote the Science Research Council about his application for a research grant. In their reply the Council assured him that his application would be considered at the next meeting of the Council's sub-committee.

Note that there are words that have a limited sense as well as a broader sense, e.g. government and Government. The logical answer is that the word with the limited sense should be given the capital. Here are a few others:

● minister and Minister; underground and Underground; state and State; powers and Powers.

If you think carefully about these examples, it is surely logical that the word with the *limited* sense is given a capital. You should at least be consistent in your treatment of capitals.

Italics

This accessory is used to give emphasis or importance. Italics are also used for contrast to indicate titles of books, newspapers and such like, foreign words and phrases, and quotations. These are some examples:

● There are *three* accessories to punctuation: *capitals, italics,* and *quotation marks*.

● A week later, *at the end of September*, she handed in her resignation.

● I read it in *The Daily Telegraph*.

● We went up to town last week to see *Ipi Tombi*, the all-black South African musical.

● The words *algebra* and *mufti* both come from Arabic.

● *An hour at your desk, a minute on your feet*, was Churchill's advice to ambitious young orators.

Note that in writing italics are shown by underlining the stressed word or phrase; on the printed page, they are shown in *italic* type.

Quotation marks

These are sometimes called inverted commas. People tend to make their use more difficult than need be. They are used:

a to enclose the *actual* words spoken, as in:
  ● Speaking with obvious sincerity he said, 'I shall never forget your kindness.'
b in quotations
  ● 'A rose by any other name would seem as sweet'. (Shakespeare)
c when mentioning the title of a book or a play or a publication
  ● She read it in 'The Straits Times'.

The real difficulty arises, perhaps, over the question of whether to use double or single quotes. Is there a difference that matters? Not really. Some writers prefer double, others prefer single. Whatever the choice, the important point to remember is consistency. Do not chop and change between the two.

Some final points on punctuation

1 Try to remember, when using points of punctuation, that they carry emphasis in the following descending degree:
  ● full stop; colon; semicolon; dash; comma.
  If you keep this pattern in mind you will not make many errors of punctuation.

2 There can be no exact rules for the use of punctuation. Try, therefore, to base your punctuation on the framework of the written word and phrase, not on the breaks for breath.

3 In business—and in most forms of communication—the trend today is to use only sufficient punctuation to keep the meaning accurate, clear, and concise. Study this example:
  ● When you were in London in June, we did agree, I think, that 10 January would be a suitable delivery date and, whilst I can scarcely argue, in view of the quantity of unsaleable stock of the current edition, that a month or two will make much difference, nevertheless, I feel that the sooner we publish the better.
  Now look at it written with the minimum of punctuation:
  ● When you were in London in June we did agree, I think, that 10 January would be a suitable delivery date and whilst I can

scarcely argue, in view of the quantity of unsaleable stock of the current edition, that a month or two will make much difference, nevertheless I feel that the sooner we publish the better.

If you read this passage aloud I think you will agree that, with its three fewer commas, it is a more compact and free-flowing passage than the first.

Exercise

Punctuate the following:

1   The point surely is this does the committee intend to consider an increase in the auditors fee if so by what amount meantime until this question has been discussed in committee nothing can be done it would be of benefit perhaps to call a meeting as soon as possible which day next week would be convenient

2   Can you tell me he asked why we havent seen you for weeks

3   These are the things you will have to provide for the expedition food warm clothing tents cooking stoves blankets and make sure theyre at the quay in good time

4   Halt who goes there

5   Further to yesterdays telephone call I enclose a note of the fee payable namely £4.50

6   It has been announced that a number of large industrial plants including an aluminium smelter a steel mill and a steel fabrication complex are to be built at jebel ali dubais second airport will be built nearby and the opportunities for contractors are likely to be considerable if events go as expected for some years to come

7   Enterprise energy enthusiasm these are basic requirements for success in any undertaking

8   The notice read gone to lunch back at 2.30

9   The typist finds mr browns reports very hard to decipher his as and us are so much alike

10   I do not have a qualification however in a foreign language but I do have two a levels and five o levels in addition to advanced certificates in both typewriting and shorthand

3 The words we use

Spelling

Why is the spelling of English so awkward and so difficult? There are possibly two reasons. The English language has many more sounds in it than letters. Because of this some of its letters do a double task, representing more than one sound. In the words pate and pat, for instance, the letter a carries two different sounds; in poke and pot the letter o differs very much in sound.

Consonants as well as vowels carry varying sounds, e.g. cake and cinema where the c is first hard, then soft in sound. Note also the difference in the g sounds in give and gem.

English is a mongrel language. It has benefited from many invaders of different nationalities. The Vikings, Saxons, Romans, and Normans have all contributed their share to the language. This fact alone accounts for many difficulties in spelling and pronunciation. Dough, cough, enough, for instance, are Anglo-Saxon in origin; all are pronounced differently, though each is spelt -ough. Mile and century and the names of the months we owe to the Romans, whereas bottle, boat, and flower all come from the French.

Naturally enough, we have borrowed extensively from Rome and Greece, but our greatest debt of all, perhaps, is to the French. We have borrowed from the languages of India, from Holland, and from Spain, from the Persians and from the Arabs, from Japan and China, even from the North American Indians. Here are some words which we have borrowed:

treacle, plumber, dentist, artist; iota, asbestos, agony, helicopter; moustache, portmanteau, machine, ballet, tableau; khaki, topi, bungalow, shampoo, thug; boss, buoy, dock, skipper; potato, chocolate, cannibal; shawl, tulip, divan; zero, algebra, alcohol, alcove; kimono, jujitsu; kowtow, pidgin; moccasin, totem.

These are but a few. If you look through your dictionary you will find a host of others from all around the world.

This diversity in the English language makes it difficult to lay down hard and fast spelling rules. Nevertheless, there are various ways by which you can overcome your spelling difficulties, for example:

1 Learn the 200 most commonly misspelt words listed in this chapter.
2 Learn the more common prefixes and suffixes.
3 Make yourself familiar with some of the more simple spelling rules.
4 Consult a dictionary when in doubt.

Correct spelling is an essential requirement for accurate communication. Words are the tools we use to express our ideas. Like all tools they are valuable only when used correctly. It is not enough to add a long list of correctly spelled words to your vocabulary. They need exercise.

Some students of language argue that punctuation is more important than spelling. On the other hand, look at this extract from Martin Higham's article on 'Letters of Application' in *The Graduate: Jobs and Courses*:

> Watch your spelling; if in doubt consult the dictionary you bought and have hardly opened. Some employers—or at least those who have read applications—are obsessional about spelling. If you really want a job with them, then play the spelling game according to the rules.

You will, of course, have to make up your own mind about this; but it can certainly do no harm to cultivate accuracy of spelling.

Now look at some of the rules to help you.

Prefixes

A **prefix** is the verbal element placed at the beginning of a word to qualify its meaning. The following are some of the more common:

Ante- and Anti-

The prefix *ante-* means before, as in:

  antecedent   antechamber   antedate   anteroom

The prefix *anti-* means against, as in:

  anticlimax   antipathy   antiseptic
  antidote   antipodes   antisocial

Dis-, Un-, Mis-

Study these words—disappoint, unclean, mistake. In each case a prefix, *dis-, un-, mis-* has been added to its word, appoint, clean, take, without any change being made to the word. If, however, the word begins with the same letter as the last letter of the prefix, then there must be a double consonant. For example:

dissatisfied	ennoble	innumerable
dissertation	illegible	misshapen
dissipate	illicit	misspell
dissolve	immodest	unnatural

For- and Fore-

The prefixes *for-* and *fore-* need careful attention. *For-* often implies a prohibition or abstention, *fore-* means before. In this group, therefore, be guided by the meaning.

forbade	forebode
forborne	forehead
forgiveness	forerunner
forsake	forestall
forswear	foretell

Remember: *forgo* means to go without and *forego* means to go before.

Con-, Com-, Col-, Cor-

The Latin prefix *cum*, meaning with, is at the root of these prefixes, though it has suffered a slight change in each instance. In each case the third letter of the prefix agrees with the first consonant of the root word. For example:

connive	commit	collect	correct
connect	commune	collusion	corrode
connote	commodious	collapse	correspond
connoisseur	commend	collaborate	correlate

Pre-, Pro-, Per-

These call for very careful pronunciation so that their correct meaning and usage can be easily understood. There is a wealth of difference in meaning between the following pairs:

prescribe; proscribe   precede; proceed
prefer; proffer   persecute; prosecute

Suffixes or terminations

-able and -ible

The final e is usually dropped before -*able* and -*ible*. The following are examples:

conceivable   excitable   collapsible   producible
dissolvable   movable   forcible   reducible

There are always exceptions to the rule, and with words ending in *able* and -*ible* the exceptions are quite often in those words ending in g or c, where the e is retained to give the soft sound. For instance:

changeable   noticeable
manageable   peaceable
marriageable   serviceable

Further exceptions are—rateable, saleable.

-ary, -ery, -ory, -ry

It is easy to get confused over the spelling of words with these endings. The only thing to do is to learn them.

-ary	-ery	-ory	-ry
boundary	cemetery	advisory	foundry
secretary	imagery	desultory	idolatry
sedentary	monastery	dormitory	sentry

Especially confusing are stationery, the noun meaning paper, etc., and stationary, the adjective meaning fixed or motionless.

-ar, -er, -or, -ur, -re

Words with these endings are also easy to confuse. Again, the only solution to the problem is to learn the words. A particularly typical mistake is the spelling of metre and meter. The fully decimal-conscious secretary should never make the mistake of spelling metre, the measurement, as meter, the measurer. Some examples are:

-ar	-er	-or	-ur & -re
beggar	barometer	auditor	murmur
grammar	heifer	author	sulphur
muscular	traveller	councillor	theatre
singular	labourer	doctor	spectre

-ceed, -cede, -ede

Again, observation of each word is the best way of mastering its spelling. Learn the words in the table below.

-ceed	-cede	-ede
exceed	accede	impede
proceed	concede	recede
succeed	intercede	supersede

-our and -or

Do not use the American -or in words like honour, labour, favour. Note these, however:

clamour; clamorous
honour; honourable; honorary; honorarium
humour; humorous
vigour; vigorous

-fer and -cur

When the syllable -fer is to be stressed and is followed by a vowel, the r must be doubled. For example:

confer; conference; conferred; conferring
defer; deference; deferred; deferring
prefer; preference; preferred; preferring
refer; reference; referee; referred; referring

The same applies to words ending in -cur, for example:

concur; concurring; concurred; concurrence
demur; demurring; demurred; demurrage
occur; occurring; occurred; occurrence
recur; recurring; recurred; recurrence; recurrent

If the r is not doubled before a following vowel, the u will sound like the u in secured.

The double l

Mistakes often occur when -*ed* and -*ing* are added to verbs ending in l. The rule is:

Double the l if it is preceded by a single vowel, as in:
    compel; compelling   control; controlled
but if it is preceded by a pair of vowels, the l is not doubled, as in:
    wail; wailing   hail; hailed

The silent letter

In English we have to cope with a mass of words containing silent letters, e.g. the silent b, the silent c, the silent g, and others. Take care with these words. Here are some. Learn them.

b	bomber	comb	debt	doubt	subtle
c	crescent	rescind	sceptre	science	scissors
g	assign	deign	foreign	gnaw	sovereign
h	hour	honest	rhyme	ghost	shepherd
gh	bright	fight	bough	eight	daughter
k	knee	knit	know	knot	knock
n	column	condemn	solemn	hymn	autumn
p	pneumonia	receipt	psalm	pseudonym	psychology
t	Christmas	fasten	listen	whistle	mortgage
w	wreck	answer	write	wrist	wrong

Adverbs

When an adverb is formed from an adjective ending in l, this l is doubled, e.g.
    special; specially   general; generally
but an adverb formed from an adjective already ending in double l does not need a third l, e.g.
    dully, fully
When an adverb is formed from an adjective ending in -*ic*, *ally* is added, e.g.
    basically, specifically, heroically
Note the exception, publicly.
    Note the spelling of wholly, truly, and duly formed from the adjectives whole, true, and due.

Nouns and verbs

In some pairs of words the verb is spelt with an s and the noun with a c; learn not to confuse these.

Verbs: license, practise, advise, devise, prophesy.
Nouns: licence, practice, advice, device, prophecy.

i before e except after c

This is a good rule, but remember that it applies only when the ie and ei rhyme with key. Here are some examples:

achieve	liege	ceiling
believe	piece	conceive
brief	shriek	deceive
chief	siege	perceive
grieve	thief	receipt

Note that in the third column the order is e before i because they follow the c. When ie and ei have any sound other than that of key, the order is ei as in:

deign	freight	inveigle	rein
eider	heifer	leisure	skein
eight	heighten	neigh	sleigh
feint	heir	obeisance	sleight

Foreign plurals

Some words always keep their foreign plurals. For example:

Singular	Plural	Singular	Plural
agendum	agenda	memorandum	memoranda
bureau	bureaux	minimum	minima
crisis	crises	oasis	oases
criterion	criteria	phenomenon	phenomena
datum	data	thesis	theses
erratum	errata	tableau	tableaux
hypothesis	hypotheses		

Some words have an English plural as well as a foreign plural form, e.g. formulas and formulae; appendixes and appendices.

If in doubt prefer an English plural to a doubtful foreign plural.

Latin words

We talk and write and know pure Latin much more than we realise. Probably few of us appreciate how many Latin survivals there are or how familiar they are in use. Look at some of these words and phrases; they are pure Latin, but are now hardly ever recognised as such—so much so, in fact, that they need no indication in writing by italics or quotation marks.

addendum	genius	pro rata
agenda	gratis	quantum
alia	impedimenta	quasi
alibi	in camera	quorum
alma mater	index	quota
anno domini	inter alia	ratio
bona fide	interim	regalia
bonus	janitor	requiem
censor	magnum	status quo
colossus	major	stratum
crux	maximum	subpoena
curriculum	memento	terminus
data	minimum	ultimatum
dictum	minor	vacuum
et cetera (etc.)	omnibus	verbatim
exit	opus	vice versa
extempore	par	vim
finis	post (after)	viva

This list could be trebled and still would not cover all the pure Latin words used in everyday conversation and writing.

In addition to this list, there are a great number of Latin phrases and quotations which, although not so widely understood, are necessary to our language because they have never been effectively translated for casual use. It has not been possible to improve on them; they convey what is meant more briefly and forcibly than the equivalent English expressions. Here are just a few:

annus mirabilis	a year of wonders
casus belli	a cause for war
compos mentis	of sound mind
de facto	by virtue of the fact
ex libris	from the books of
ex officio	by virtue of his office
in situ	in the position

ipso facto	by the fact or deed referred to
persona grata	a welcome person
prima facie	at first sight; on the face of it
quid pro quo	value for value

Using the dictionary

The dictionary can be your lifeline. It should never be far away from you. How do you read it? Here, three of its readings are simplified.

cōali′tion, *n.* Union, fusion; temporary combination for special ends between parties that retain distinctive principles. [f. L *coalitio*]

mea′gre, *a.* (Of persons etc.) lean, thin; poor, scanty; (of literary composition, ideas, etc.) wanting in fullness. [f. OF *maigre* f. L *macer -cri*]

ram′ble, *v.i.*, & *n.* **1.** Walk (*v.* & *n.*) for pleasure & without definite route. **2.** Wander in discourse, talk or write disconnectedly. [?]

To understand these definitions, follow these guides when reading your dictionary:

1 The words defined (coalition, meagre, ramble) are shown in heavy type and are listed in alphabetical order.

2 Accented syllables are followed by the accent mark ′; short vowels are shown by the sign ˘; long vowels are shown by the sign ¯.

3 Small letters (*n, a, v*) show the part of speech, namely: noun, adjective, verb.

4 The derivation or origin of the word is shown in square brackets. In the above examples it is Latin, Old French, and unknown.

You will find at the beginning of your dictionary a list of all abbreviations used. When in doubt you should consult this list. Remember: when more than one meaning is given for a word, e.g. **ramble**, take care to select the meaning which fits the sense.

You cannot over-use your dictionary.

Here is a list of two hundred words; it constitutes a quarter of the more commonly misspelt words in our language.

absence	acquainted	agreeable	Antarctic	Arctic
accidentally	addresses	all right	anxiety	argument
accommodate	aerial	amateur	apparent	arrangement
achieved	aggravate	among	appearance	ascend
acknowledge	aggregate	analysis	appropriate	athletic

automation	disastrous	height	occasional	recognise
awful	discipline	heroes	occasionally	recommended
bachelor	dissatisfied	honorary	occurred	referred
beginning	efficiency	humorous	occurrence	relieved
believed	eighth	hungry	omitted	repetition
benefited	eliminated	hurriedly	omission	restaurant
beneficial	embarrassed	hypocrisy	opinion	rhythm
breathe	emphasise	imagination	originally	scarcely
budgeted	enthusiasm	immediately	parallel	secretaries
business	equipped	immigrate	parliament	seize
ceiling	especially	incidentally	pastime	sentence
certain	essential	independent	permanent	separate
choice	exaggerated	indispensable	permissible	severely
clothes	excellent	influential	perseverance	shining
college	exercise	intelligence	personnel	similar
colleagues	exhausted	irresistible	physical	sincerely
coming	existence	knowledge	planning	statutory
committee	expenses	liaison	pleasant	successful
comparative	experience	literature	possesses	supersede
competent	extremely	livelihood	preceding	suppression
completely	familiar	lose	preference	surprising
conscientious	February	losing	prejudice	synonym
conscious	financial	lying	preliminary	tendency
consistent	foreign	maintenance	prestige	tragedy
convenience	forty	marriage	privilege	transferred
courteous	friend	medicine	procedure	twelfth
courtesy	fulfilled	Mediterranean	proceeds	unconscious
criticism	gauge	miniature	professional	undoubtedly
deceive	genius	minutes	professor	unnecessary
decision	government	mischievous	pronunciation	until
definite	grammar	murmur	proprietary	usually
desirable	grievance	necessary	psychology	valuable
desperate	guard	negotiate	quiet	view
disappeared	guardian	niece	really	Wednesday
disappointed	handkerchief	noticeable	received	woollen

Now look at this more difficult list:

abeyance	chromium	deficit	extraordinary	liquidate
accentuate	circumspect	deteriorate	faculty	manuscript
accustomed	coherent	differentiate	fluctuate	mechanism
administer	comparable	directory	forbearance	mediocre
advantageous	component	discrepancy	fundamental	paragraph
annuity	comprehensive	discriminate	generous	performance
anomaly	conditional	disparity	graduate	potential
artificial	confidential	dubious	ideal	prejudicial
auctioneer	considerate	elementary	immaculate	priority
belated	consolidate	employee	implicate	probability
bilingual	contemporary	encourage	indemnify	proportionate
brevity	contingency	enumerate	initiate	quandary
brochure	contradictory	envisage	innumerable	questionable
canvass	corporate	equivalent	insignificant	rational
capacity	corroborate	exceptional	installation	recipient
casualty	credentials	exorbitant	intercept	registrar
catalogue	customary	expedient	inventory	regulate
characteristic	defective	explanatory	likelihood	reinstate

relevant	scarcity	standardise	supplementary	utilitarian
remarkable	significance	statistics	telegram	vacancy
representative	solution	substantiate	temporary	versatile
requisite	sophisticated	suitability	theory	vicinity
reservation	spectacular	superfluous	traditional	vindicate
respective	speculate			

Master these words and their meaning with the help of your dictionary for you will meet most of them when writing business letters.

Exercise

1 Write sentences to show the meaning of the following words:

asterisk; auxiliary; collusion; connote; deign; ennoble; feint; foreboding; forego; inveigle; proffer; proscribe.

2 Form the negatives of the following words by adding prefixes:

allow; favour; important; known; legal; lovely; loyal; noble; regular; reverence; trust; trustworthy.

3 Use the following words in sentences to show what they mean:

abridgment; contagious; contention; discrepancy; fallacious; honorarium; intercede; lucid; perceptible; privilege; prohibitive.

4 Using these endings, *-ar, -er, -or, -ur, -re* complete the following words and give the meaning in each case:

aggress . .	counsell . .	lem . .
aug . .	hydromet . .	massac . .
cens . .	inc . .	somb . .
conjur . .	jur . .	tuss . .

5 Explain the meanings of:

device; devise; licence; license.

6 Introduce the following words into sentences:

commission; condescend; indefinite; omission; precedence; recompense; temporarily.

7 Explain the meanings of:

allergic; intrinsic; philanthropic; psychic; soporific.

8 Differentiate between these pairs of words by using them in sentences:

collision; collusion   proceed; precede
human; humane   practice; practise

9 Explain the following phrases and then use each of them correctly in a sentence:

established fact   poetic licence
incidental expenses   press release
interested party   secondary meaning
mass production   special edition
passive resistance   standard performance

10 Give the plural of the following:

analysis; axis; erratum; focus; index; medium; radius; species; stamen; stratum; terminus.

4 Accuracy of expression

In all writing accuracy of expression is important. It is a good idea to build up a wide and accurate vocabulary, adding to it new words when the opportunity occurs, but guard against using such words solely for effect; this will only result in stilted and awkward expression.

When you come across an unfamiliar word, refer to a dictionary and memorise the exact meaning of the word, its proper pronunciation and its part of speech so that you will know how to use it correctly.

Synonyms

The dictionary gives this definition: one or more words having the same or nearly the same essential meaning. Here are some examples:

grand; majestic   task; work; duty
battle; conflict   acute; keen; sharp
amiable; friendly   state; condition; circumstance

Sometimes pairs of words seem identical in meaning, but closer examination reveals a distinction not at first apparent, for example: wealthy; rich. Wealthy applied to a person means having great possessions, owning wealth. It can also be applied to a country, meaning prosperous. Rich, while indicating wealth, may also be applied to the following, though with a different meaning in each instance:

rich soil: fertile soil
rich food: full of nutritious content
rich quality: top-grade (superior quality)

It is obvious, therefore, that you must be careful in your use of synonyms. Look at the following:
- Why do you *hesitate* to agree when you know you have no option?
- The Chairman continued to *vacillate* on the question of salary for the new branch manager.

● Under the constant barrage of questions the witness's certainty began to *waver*.

In these three sentences each synonym has a slightly different meaning.

With the help of a dictionary study the following synonyms and note that in some cases the words have a secondary meaning:

achieve; accomplish; gain; perform
conformity; likeness; similarity
accident; chance; contingency
emergency; exigency; necessity
conspicuous; distinguished; eminent

Antonyms

These are words which are opposite in meaning. For example:

good; bad	genuine; false
white; black	joy; sorrow
guilt; innocence	miserly; prodigal

Homonyms

A homonym is a word having the same pronunciation as another but differing from it in origin, meaning and, often, in spelling, e.g.

bare; bear	meet; meat
pail; pale	site; cite
seem; seam	maid; made

It will help you to remember the different meanings of synonym, antonym, and homonym if you understand their Greek derivations:

syn	with	*homo*	same
anti	against, opposite	*onym*	name

Pairs of words

Learn to differentiate between words that look alike or sound alike. Close observation, practice, and the use of your dictionary is the only way to master them. Take allusion and illusion for example:

Allusion means an indirect reference, as in:
- In his report to the police the taxi-driver alluded several times to the behaviour of his passengers.

Illusion means a false impression or image, as in:
- Joan thought herself ugly, an illusion not shared by her friends.

Here are some more pairs:

adverse; averse   depreciate; deprecate
affect; effect   illicit; elicit
council; counsel   principle; principal

Use of prepositions

Prepositions are usually short words: to, at, of, for, about, in. These show the relationship of one thing or person to another. For example:
- The book is *on* the table.
- The sandwiches are *in* the basket.
- She was popular *among* her colleagues.

We are sometimes careless in their use. Too often we say accompanied with instead of *by*, or different to when it should be different *from*, as in these examples:
- She was accompanied *by* her father.

This is the correct preposition to use after accompanied.
- The outcome was quite different to what I expected.

This is incorrect; it should be:
- The outcome was quite different *from* what I expected.

To help you, here is a list of words with their correct prepositions.

agree *with* a person
agree *to* a proposal or plan
averse *to* a plan or suggestion
collaborate *with* a person
comply *with* a request
consequent *upon* an action
correspond *with* a person
correspond *to* (one thing may correspond *to* another)
deficient *in* knowledge, etc.
defer *to* a person's viewpoint or wish
distaste *for* an action, situation or thing
entrust *to* a person
entrust *with* a thing

    indifferent *to* criticism, a person or a situation
    impatient *with* a person
    impatient *of* authority, control
    negligent *of* duty
    responsible *for* an action
    responsible *to* a person
    relevant *to* a discussion, point of view
    preferable *to* a person or thing
    prevail *upon* (*on*) a person
    substitute *for* a person or thing

Exercise

1   Give antonyms for:

    general; smooth; ugly; democratic; obscure; masterful.

2   Use the following homonyms in sentences to show their differ-
    ences in meaning:

    reel; real   serial; cereal   bough; bow.

3   Show the difference between these pairs of words by using them
    in sentences:

    practice, practise; dependent, dependant; intervene, interfere;
    continuous, continual; compliment, complement.

4   Find a synonym to replace each of the following:

    a not loud enough to be heard
    b siding neither with one person nor the other
    c on the spur of the moment
    d optimistic
    e a person's life-story written by himself

5   Show in a sentence the preposition(s) to be used after:

    affinity; abstain; compensate; responsible; instil; essential.

Common grammatical errors

It will help your English if you recognise some errors which are easy
to make; you can then guard against them. Here are some of the
more common.

The collective noun

This is the name given to a group or collection of people or things, for example: committee, staff, flock, community, audience.

Collective nouns take a singular verb. This is sometimes forgotten when the subject is separated from the verb by several words or phrases. For example:

● The bundle of books, magazines and papers were lying on the table.

Here the plural verb were is wrong because the subject word bundle is singular; the verb must therefore be in the singular:

● The bundle of books, magazines and papers *was* lying on the table.

In some instances a collective noun may take a plural verb. This happens when the stress is on the individual items making up the collective noun rather than on the collective noun itself, e.g.

● The committee *was* unanimous when it came to voting.

But:

● The committee of directors *were* unanimous when it came to voting.

That and which

That restricts the meaning of the word it defines; **which** does not. These examples will show the difference.

● The typewriter *that* needs repair is in the cupboard.

Here, the word that tells us which typewriter is in the cupboard—it is the one that needs repair; 'that', therefore, is restrictive.

● The typewriter, *which* needs repair, is in the cupboard.

The use of which, with commas, changes the meaning. Here, the implication is that there is only one typewriter—it needs repair and is in the cupboard.

We tend, however, to use that and which somewhat indiscriminately, especially in our spoken language.

The unrelated relative pronoun

This is one of the most common of all grammatical errors. Remember that the relative pronoun must have an antecedent: something it refers back to. You must therefore give it one or recast the sentence. For example:

● They did not have a quorum for the meeting which meant it had to be cancelled.

Ask yourself: does which refer back to anything? No: therefore the sentence must be recast in some way:

- They did not have a quorum for the meeting so, because of this, the meeting had to be cancelled, or
- They did not have a quorum for the meeting; therefore, it had to be cancelled.

Me

This little word causes trouble. Do not be afraid of it. Try to remember that it is an object word. Take this sentence:

- They were at the station to meet John and me.

This is correct because me is the object word after the verb to meet. It would be wrong to say John and I here, because I is always a subject word and in the sentence, me is the object word after to meet.

Remember that a noun or pronoun which is dependent on a preposition becomes an object word. Particular care must be taken when two persons (or pronouns) occur after a preposition, e.g.

- It will be impossible for you and I.

This is wrong. It ought to be:

- It will be impossible for you and *me*.

Note that the pronoun me is the object word after for.

Similarly, between him and I is incorrect: it ought to be between *him* and *me*, because both him and me are object words after the preposition between.

The verb 'to be'

People tend to be careless in its use. Remember that the verb to be must link nouns and pronouns (persons) which have the same relationship to each other e.g.

- It is me ought to be It is *I*.

It is the subject and I is really an extension of the subject. It must follow the relationship rule of the verb to be. Therefore me is incorrect because it is the object word.

Degrees of comparison

An adjective has three degrees. The simple adjective is said to be positive—*sweet*; the adjective used to compare two objects is comparative—*sweeter*; and the adjective used to compare three or more things is superlative—*sweetest*.

It is important to recognise these degrees. A very common error is to use the superlative degree when only two things are being compared. For example:

- Which is your weakest eye? ought to be Which is your *weaker* eye?

because only two eyes are being compared. Similarly:

- This essay is the best of the two, should be This essay is the *better* of the two

because better is used to compare two items.

The dangling participle

This, more correctly, is called the misrelated participle. The present or past participle is used frequently when opening a sentence, but care should be taken for, used wrongly, it can lead to oddities of expression.

Remember that the participle must extend the subject word or words of the sentence, for example:

- *Jumping* on the moving bus, *the old man* missed the step and was dragged along the street.

Here the opening participle jumping is correctly used. The word jumping extends or describes the subject of the sentence, the old man.

Here are some more examples of dangling or misrelated participles:

- Walking through the town, the streets looked deserted.

This is wrong because it suggests that the streets were walking through the town and this, of course, is nonsense. It can be corrected by changing the subject word to we in order to make sense. The sentence now becomes:

- *Walking* through the town, *we* found the streets deserted.

Can you spot the error in the following sentence?

- Seated in the train, the time seemed to us to pass almost too quickly.

Seated is an extension which should tell us about the time, but time, of course, could not be sitting in the train. Sense can be made of the sentence by getting rid of the participle seated in this way:

- *As we sat* in the train, the time seemed to us to pass almost too quickly.

Note: you can often correct a misrelated participle by turning the sentence upside down, for example:

- Being a fine day, we went on a picnic.

Here the participle being does not extend the subject we. It is

wrong and therefore bad English. The sentence should be corrected
in this way:

- The day being fine, we went on a picnic.

The dangling participle is one of the more common errors of
expression. The examples given should help you to eradicate it from
your writing.

The end preposition

A preposition should not end a sentence:

- Who are you looking for? should be *For whom* are you looking?
- What book does that passage come from? should be *From what*
  book does that passage come?

Do not, however, forget Churchill's very firm protest against the
re-positioning of one of his prepositions in reply to one of his
succinct memoranda—'This is an insult up with which I will not
put.' So perhaps, thanks to Sir Winston, we should not be too
dogmatic about the rule of the end preposition.

The split infinitive

What is it, and when can it be justified? A **split infinitive** is simply
the placing of an adverb between the preposition to and the verb.
Thus, to clearly understand is a split infinitive; to understand
clearly, is not.

Nevertheless, we distort a sentence much too often in order to
avoid a split infinitive which does not even exist, and we produce a
monstrosity like this:

- He was proposed as a candidate likely generally to be accepted.

under the delusion that we shall split an infinitive if we write:

- He was proposed as a candidate likely to be generally accepted.

The infinitive is complete in 'to be'; the participle accepted is not
part of it.

The difficulty of the split infinitive becomes greater when dealing
simply with a verb and an adverb. For example:

- *To* considerably *improve* the present wages of the teachers

might just as well be written

- *To improve* the present wages of the teachers considerably

thus avoiding a split infinitive. But—and it is an important but—if
the split infinitive is avoided in this example, some of the force and
clarity of the adverb considerably is lost.

As a general guide infinitives may be split when to leave them unsplit results in ambiguity. For example:

● Now that we are in the Common Market we have a right to expect the other Market members *to* at least *consider* our interests.

This is a good example of the justifiable split infinitive. Look at it more closely. If at least is put before to, then at least would belong with other Market members, which is not the meaning of the statement. If it is put at the end after interests, it would then belong either to interests or to to consider our interests, neither of which is intended. Where it stands (between to and consider) it stands positively with complete clarity of emphasis and meaning.

No longer should the split infinitive be seen as a verbal crime; it can be both justified and grammatically correct.

The perfect (past) infinitive

What is wrong with this sentence?

● He expected to have seen Mr Brown yesterday.

The expecting and the seeing were to take place on the same day. It is unnecessary to use to have seen. The sentence should read:

● He expected *to see* Mr Brown yesterday.

Here is another example:

● I hoped to have gone with you today.

This should be simplified as follows:

● I hoped *to go* with you today.

Shall and will

These two helping verbs, indicating future tense or time, are conjugated in this way:

	Singular	Plural
First person	I shall	We shall
Second person	You will	You will
Third person	He, she, it will	They will

Used like this, they indicate simple futurity. To indicate something more emphatic than intention, to convey the idea of purpose and determination, command or threat, the conjugation is reversed:

	Singular	Plural
First person	I will	We will
Second person	You shall	You shall
Third person	He, she, it shall	They shall

I *shall* be there is a simple promise of future intention; but I *will* be there indicates my intention to allow nothing to prevent my attendance. They *will* follow us to the station is a statement of what is expected; but they *shall* follow us expresses a threat of rebuke in the case of failure to follow. You *shall* not steal is a command, very different from you *will* not steal.

In questions, shall and will carry fine distinctions of meaning:

- Shall we go? means Do you wish us to go?
- Will you go? means Do you intend to go?
- Shall you go? means Is there any likelihood of your going?
- Will she go? means Is it likely she will go?

Note, however, that in conversation the words shall and will are seldom used precisely.

May and can

Very often can is used wrongly instead of may. **Can** simply means ability to do; **may** implies permission.

- Can I bring John back to tea? should be *May* I bring John back to tea?

Can is used correctly in this sentence:

- *Can* you lift this table?

Should and would

The same rule applies here as applied to shall and will. When the past tense is used, should normally replaces shall and would replaces will. Thus we do not say I *shall* be glad if you *would* do this, but I *should* be glad if you *would* do this.

Note carefully the following uses:

1 'We shall be pleased if you will' is used when a request is being made for something which we have a right to expect, e.g.

- We shall be pleased if you will let us have your cheque without further delay.
- We shall be pleased if you will replace the damaged bookcase before the end of next week.

2 'We should be pleased if you would (or could)' is used when a favour is being asked, e.g.

- We should be pleased if you would let us know whether they pay accounts promptly.
- We should be pleased if you could reduce your quotation in view of the competition we have to face.

Remember that *should* is used for all three persons—I, you, he, she, it, we, they—when duty or obligation is implied. For example:
- He *should* accept the result, but I cannot say whether he will.

Exercise

Correct these sentences and give reasons for your corrections.

1 This house is the most attractive of the two, but any of them would suit us.

2 Talking at such a speed, the subject was too involved for me to easily grasp.

3 I hoped to have gone with you to the meeting but, between you and I, I could not afford the time.

4 Checking the figures carefully, the clerk's mistake was soon discovered by the manager.

5 I am determined that this item will be discussed.

6 Though not wishing to insist upon it, this point deserves consideration.

7 He shall be taking his seat on the board next month.

8 I should like to have seen them again before I leave.

9 This collection of pens, pencils, and books are cluttering up the desk.

10 Between you and I, I think the decision is a bad one.

11 This is the most unkindest view of all.

12 The committee are divided in their view.

Words misplaced and misused

The position of a word may change the meaning of a phrase or sentence completely. There are many instances of this, but the most common misplacement is that of only. Look at this example:
- This card is not transferable and may only be used by the person named on it.

This should read:

- This card is not transferable and may be used *only* by the person named on it.

In this example only is restrictive on the person (as intended) rather than on the verb.

Another example is:

- I only saw him last week.

Here only saw suggests that I did not speak to him or acknowledge him. The word only should really explain or add to the meaning of last week; the sentence should therefore be:

- I saw him *only* last week.

Remember that only must be next to the word it explains.

Look carefully at a few examples of misplacements:

- He has not only shown himself to be discourteous but also careless in his attitude to work.

Here not only is out of position and should come immediately before discourteous—the word it qualifies or explains:

- He has shown himself to be *not only* discourteous *but also* careless in his attitude to work.
- The flight is either scheduled for 1300 or 1400 hours.

The word either is in the wrong place; it should come before 1300 i.e. the word or words it is explaining:

- The flight is scheduled for *either* 1300 *or* 1400 hours.

Many of the words, phrases, and expressions we use are not so much bad English as bad style; in other words, commonplaces of careless writing. Correcting them does not necessarily involve replacing one word or one expression by another word or expression, but rather understanding the use and meaning of the word you want to use.

The following words and expressions are not set down in any significant order; they are listed alphabetically for easy reference.

Aggravate and irritate

Aggravate means to add to some already troublesome condition or matter, as in:

- His arthritis was aggravated by the severe winter.

Irritate means to annoy:

- She irritates me with her constant chatter.

Alternative

This word is constantly misused. Often it is used to refer to choice. Remember that choice can apply to any number; but **alternative** refers to only *two* possible decisions, courses of action, situations, etc. Look at these examples:

- The *alternative* is an immediate cancellation of the project or its indefinite postponement.
- We have the *choice* of appointing Mr Jones, reconsidering some of the other applicants, or readvertising the post.
- The *alternative* is to sell the property.
- I had no *alternative*.

All these examples show the correct use of the word.

Among and between

Among is used when two or more persons or things are involved.
- I divided the sweets among the three boys.

Between is used when only two things are involved, as in:
- There was little to choose between the two applicants.

Note, however, that when more than two are involved but each is considered individually, between should be used in preference to among, for example:

- The solicitor drew up an agreement *between* the four trustees.

The use of between here is correct because the four trustees are being considered individually.

And/or

This was originally meant to be a short cut to an alternative decision. It has, in fact, become the reverse—an ambiguity. For example:

- If, in supermarkets, there was an agreed trust system, how much would this decrease the cheating and/or stealing?

What is meant here is the cheating *and* the stealing. The word or has no place in this context.

Look at another example:

- Proposals will be welcomed from management and/or work force.

This should read:

- Proposals will be welcomed both from the management and from the work force.

And/or has no place in our writing.

Anticipate

This word means to forestall, to be beforehand with something, as in:

- Your letter of 27 June has anticipated an enquiry we were about to make.

In this sentence, however, it is wrongly used to mean expect:

- She anticipated that he would look older.

It should be:

- She *expected* that he would look older.

Anybody and anyone

Anybody in the sense of any person must be written as one word. Any body, written as two words, naturally means something quite different. The same applies to *everybody, somebody, nobody*, each of which is written as one word. Written as two words they have a totally different meaning, for example:

- *Every body* had been mutilated.

Similarly, anyone meaning anybody must be written as one word. Written as two it means any single person.

Appreciate

This word indicates an increase in value, as in:

- Good wine, furniture, and violins appreciate with age.

The word appreciate is often wrongly used in the sense of welcome, for example:

- We appreciate their influence for good in public life.

It should be:

- We *welcome* their influence for good in public life.

Too often it is used passively ('it will be appreciated that') instead of actively ('you will appreciate') and far too often these phrases are used as padding, as in:

- It will be appreciated that rising costs and wages have forced up the price of our motor cars.

Here the phrase has little value other than padding—so it should be omitted. Both phrases can nearly always be discarded in our writing, with little harm to the sense, but with much benefit to style.

There is another objection to the use of the word appreciate. It is more vague in meaning than the words *realise, see,* or *understand*, and for this reason alone you should use one of these three words in place of the loose appreciate.

As and like

As is a conjunction or joining word, but **like** is a comparing word and must not be used as a joining word. Study these examples:

- I wish I could sing like you do.

Here, like has been wrongly used as a joining word. The sentence should read:

- I wish I could sing *as* you do.

In this example:

- He is *like* his father.

like is used correctly because a comparison is intended.

As from

These two words are used too often—and wrongly—when the one word *from* or *since* should be used instead. For example:

- As from 1 March the mortgage rate will be raised to 14%.

This should be:

- *From* 1 March the mortgage rate will be raised to 14%.

Similarly:

- As from 1 February the rate has been $12\frac{1}{2}\%$.

Here, as from simply means since, so the word since should be used:

- *Since* 1 February the rate has been $12\frac{1}{2}\%$.

As and when

Only one of these words should be used since only one is necessary.

- As and when your proposal is accepted action will be taken.

This should be:

- *When* your proposal is accepted action will be taken.

As yet and yet

Look at this sentence:

- No plan has been arranged as yet.

As adds nothing to the meaning of the sentence; it is therefore superfluous. The sentence should be:

- No plan has *yet* been arranged.

Note the exception at the beginning of a sentence, however, where yet has a different meaning, as in:

- Yet (i.e. despite everything) the experiment has gone badly.
- As yet (i.e. up until now) the experiment has gone badly.

Study carefully the two different meanings.

Awful

This word is much abused. Look at these examples:
- April was an awful month.
- John really is an awful ass.
- Margaret was an awful sight in her new hat.

We are only justified in describing weather as awful if we are experiencing a severe thunderstorm or some other weather catastrophe which threatens life and property, and so does fill us with *awe*—and, as a result, frightens us. No person foolish enough to be described as an ass can create a feeling of awe, nor could Margaret in her new hat have been an awful sight. Awful, therefore, is used correctly only when it refers to a catastrophe or disaster, e.g.
- The burning cars and buses in the city's main square were an *awful* spectacle, an *awesome* reminder of the horror of war.

Disinterested and uninterested

These two words are often confused. To be **disinterested** in a matter is to be without self-interest in it, to be impartial. To be **uninterested** is to have no interest. For example:
- The umpire at a cricket match should be disinterested; if he were uninterested he might let his attention wander.

Disinterested implies that he should be unbiased in order to be able to make fair judgments.

Either and neither

Either is used to indicate one of an alternative, that is, one of two things:
- I do not agree with *either* of the suggestions.

Here, there are only two suggestions. Where there are more than two choices any must be used:
- I do not agree with *any* of the suggestions.

This means there are more than two suggestions.

Look at this example of the misuse of the word either in an official government form. The form called for the completion of particulars, and asked:

This should be either—
Your 65th birthday
or The day you gave up regular employment
or The date from which you wish to be treated as retired.

The word either has no place here and should be omitted.

Remember that the word either is singular and therefore must take a singular verb.

● Either Mr Brown or Mr Jones *is* to be invited.

Similarly, **neither** is used to refer to two things or persons and takes its verb in the singular.

● *Neither* of the girls *intends* coming.

This means that there are only two girls. If more than two are meant, then **none** must be used, but note that none may take a singular or plural verb, according to sense. When it means not any it may be followed by a plural verb:

● *None* of the committee *are* prepared to support the proposal.

When it means not a single one it takes a singular verb:

● *None* of the class *is* prepared to come next Wednesday.

When two singular subjects are connected by the words either . . .or, or neither . . . nor, a singular verb must be used:

● *Neither* Miss Smith *nor* Miss Black *was* present.

Etc.

This is the shortened form of the Latin et cetera meaning and other things, and the rest. Avoid using it other than at the end of a list of items given almost in full, for example:

● On his desk lay a stack of files, trade journals, newspaper cuttings, photographs, etc.

Here, etc. indicates that the list of items was very nearly complete. It also indicates that the 'and other things' were not of sufficient importance to mention separately.

If a list has been introduced by the words: for example, such as, as follows, then the addition of etc. at the end is wrong, as in:

● His desk lay cluttered under a mass of miscellaneous items, such as: files, trade journals, cuttings, photographs, reference books, etc.

Here, the addition of etc. is incorrect, and should be omitted.

In formal writing follow this simple rule: do not use etc.

However

This word is used too loosely. Too often it is placed wrongly at the beginning of a sentence, for example:

● He fell and broke an arm two weeks before the examination. However, he decided to sit the examination.

Here, however means nevertheless or despite this, and should not have been used at the beginning of the sentence.

When used other than at the beginning of a sentence, the word however can add meaning to a sentence, as in:

● I think, *however*, that we should support the Chairman's suggestion.

When however does come first it means to whatever extent, in whatever way, for example:

● *However* you try to help him, he will not take your advice.

Infer and imply

We misuse these words because not enough care has been taken to grasp their proper meaning. **Infer** means to form an opinion, to come to a conclusion. It is therefore wrong to say:

● Are you inferring that I don't know what I am talking about?

The correct word to use in this instance is *implying*. To **imply** means to hint, to suggest. The sentence should therefore read:

● Are you *implying* that I don't know what I am talking about?

Look at these four sentences:

● Your letter seems to *imply* that we have given the wrong advice.

● We can only *imply* that you are not anxious to accept our terms.

● Your *inference* is correct; the salesgirl was in fact sacked for dishonesty.

● Such an *implication* is quite unjustifiable.

One of these is incorrect. Which one? Test the two meanings and find out. The error is in the second example where imply should be infer, i.e. We can only 'come to the conclusion . . .'

Less and fewer

Take care with these two words. Less should not be used to mean fewer. Remember that **less** refers to quantity and **fewer** refers to numbers. For example:

● My problems are *less* than yours.

This means that my problems are not so great as yours.

● My problems are *fewer* than yours.

This means that my problems are less in number than yours.

Nice

This word is so over-worked that it has now lost meaning. Therefore avoid using it in any way other than correctly, namely:

- Elizabeth has a *nice* ear for music.

Here, nice means discriminating.

- That is much too *nice* a distinction to make.

Nice in this instance means subtle or delicate.

The following uses of nice are all incorrect and should not be used:

- I had a nice holiday in the Carribean; I met a nice girl; She had a nice face; Thank you for your nice letter.

Perfectly correct, however, is:

- You timed your entry *nicely*.

Nor

The use of this word needs a little care, for it is often used wrongly after a negative expression, for example:

- She cannot type efficiently nor keep files up to date.

This should be:

- She cannot type efficiently *or* keep files up to date, or
- She can *neither* type efficiently *nor* keep files up to date.

Owing to and due to

These two expressions look easy, but they are, in fact, often misused. Perhaps they are difficult to differentiate. Remember that **owing to** relates to a verb, as in:

- She failed her examination *owing to* her lack of interest.

Here, owing to relates to the verb failed. **Due to** relates to a noun, for example:

- John's failure was *due to* his lack of interest.

Due to here refers back to the noun failure.

Personally

The use of this word is often unnecessary. The dictionary states that **personally** means in person. It gives a good example: 'he conducted them personally' or 'a personally conducted tour'—that is, conducted in one's own person. Now look at this example:

- Personally, I consider it a good idea.

Here there is no need for the word personally because it adds nothing that the word I does not convey; it is merely emphasis. The sentence should read:

- I consider it a good idea.

Under or in the circumstances

Are we to say under the circumstances or in the circumstances? The meaning of circumstance is standing within a circle, so the correct expression is *in* the circumstances. *Under* the circumstances, however, is more often spoken and written than *in* the circumstances. There is a logical reason for this. In the circumstances is used when expressing a situation or a state of affairs, as in:

- *In* the circumstances I feel I cannot accept the nomination.

Under the circumstances is used when some action takes place, for example:

- *Under* the circumstances I have decided not to accept the nomination.

We should not be too dogmatic about the subtle difference between these two expressions. They are so nearly identical that both are acceptable.

While

The dictionary gives the meaning of this word as during the time that. This example, therefore, is correct:

- *While* in office as Chairman, he could not have been more considerate to his committee.

We tend, however, to use the word loosely to mean although, as in:

- While I have no experience in taking minutes, I have been secretary to several committees.

Note, however, that the use of while as an equivalent to although is permissible where the meaning is not obscure, for example:

- *While* she was an excellent typist, her manner on the telephone was much too abrupt.

The message of all these examples is that words are the means by which we seek to influence the thoughts of others—to persuade, to convince, to stimulate, to encourage, to dissuade. Used correctly, words are powerful instruments; used incorrectly, they make fools of us.

5 Find the mistakes

This chapter contains six exercises based on Chapters 2, 3 and 4. Each exercise contains errors of English—in punctuation, spelling, word order, accuracy of expression, and misuse of words, examples of which have been outlined in the previous three chapters.

The number of errors is shown within brackets. Try to find them. They are arranged in progressive grades of difficulty. The answers, with explanation where necessary, are at the end of the exercises.

Exercise one

The Chairman predicted that this year would be the very best year for the Company since the boom year of ten years' ago. He said that they have every reason to be optimistic for this year and the way that sales were increasing lead the board to think that forcasts might be on the conservative side. (7)

Exercise two

Between you and I there need be no arguements. You only see it from the viewpoint of the secretarial staff whereas I have to consider the question on three alternative issues. However, I hope to thoroughly examine the situation so that a decision can be reached briefly. (8)

Exercise three

Personally I think the idea a good one but owing to unforseen circumstances I am not prepared to accept such a decision like you infer. (6)

Exercise four

We have the choice of two candidates. We have to select the best one for the job, remembering that the work calls for tact, clear thinking and an ability to get on with people. Jones manner it seemed to me was a little aggravating while Robinson improved as his interview proggressed. (7)

Exercise five

Checking the figures carefully, the cashier's mistake was soon discovered by the manager. Either an over-sight or a wrong entry were responsible for the mistake. What was to be done. The manager was in a quandary, but he felt that action had to be taken and taken quickly. He decided that as from 1 March he would introduce a new check system. (7)

Exercise six

'All right', he said, but I cannot agree with you. Brown seems to be under the allusion that the managing director was biased. I am sure that no body else thought so. Nevertheless in fairness to Brown I must say that the Managing Director was somewhat self opinionated in his remarks, and I should have preferred him to be a little more uninterested.' (8)

Here are the answers to the exercises—as the author sees them.

Exercise one

1 *best* is already a superlative, therefore *very* is unnecessary.
2 *years'* should be *years* as it is a simple plural of year.
3 *have* should be in the past tense *had*, as it is reported speech.
4 There should be a comma before 'and'.
5 *lead* is a misspelling of *led*.
6 *board* should carry a capital 'B'.
7 *forcasts* is a misspelling of *forecasts*.

The Chairman predicted that this year would be the best year for the Company since the boom year of ten years ago. He said that they had every reason to be optimistic for this year, and the way that sales were increasing led the Board to think that forecasts might be on the conservative side.

Exercise two

1 *you and I* should read *you and me*, after the preposition between.
2 *arguement* is a misspelling of *argument*.
3 *only* is misplaced; it should come after 'it'.

4 There should be a comma after 'staff'.
5 There cannot be three *alternative* issues; the word is misused here. *Separate* issues would be better.
6 *However* is incorrect at the beginning of a sentence; replace it with *nevertheless* or write 'I hope, however, to'.
7 *to thoroughly examine* is an unacceptable split infinitive; correct it by placing thoroughly after situation.
8 *briefly* is misused; *shortly* is the correct term.

Between you and me there need be no arguments. You see it only from the viewpoint of the secretarial staff, whereas I have to consider the question on three separate issues. Nevertheless, I hope to examine the situation thoroughly so that a decision can be reached shortly.

Exercise three

1 *Personally* means in person. There is no need for it here, therefore it should be omitted.
2 There should be a comma after 'one'.
3 *owing to* is used to relate to a verb. Its use here is incorrect; it should be replaced by *due to* as this phrase relates to a noun (circumstances).
4 *unforseen* is a misspelling of *unforeseen*.
5 *like* is a comparing word and should not be used as a joining word; it should be replaced by *as*.
6 *infer* means to form an opinion, to come to a conclusion, and is therefore used wrongly here; *imply* is the correct word, meaning to suggest.

I think the idea a good one, but due to unforeseen circumstances I am not prepared to accept such a decision as you imply.

Exercise four

1 *best* is a superlative adjective used to compare three or more things; the correct word here is *better*.
2 A comma is required after 'thinking'.
3 *Jones manner* should be *Jones's manner*.
4 There should be a comma after 'manner' and another after 'me' because the phrase *it seemed to me* is parenthetical.
5 *aggravating* is used wrongly here; *irritating* is the correct word.

6   *while* is misused here; it means during the time that—and in
     certain instances, although—neither of which is correct in this
     sentence. As a replacement use *but* because contrast is intended.
7   *proggressed* is a misspelling of *progressed*.

We have the choice of two candidates. We have to select the better
one for the job, remembering that the work calls for tact, clear
thinking, and an ability to get on with people. Jones's manner, it
seemed to me, was a little irritating but Robinson improved as his
interview progressed.

Exercise five

1   *Checking the figures carefully* is a misrelated or dangling parti-
     ciple. The participle must extend the subject of the sentence (the
     cashier's mistake); here it does not. The sentence must be recast
     in some way, for example, 'Checking the figures carefully, the
     manager soon discovered the cashier's mistake'.
2   *Either . . . or* connecting two singular subjects must take a
     singular verb, therefore *were* should be *was*.
3   *over-sight* is not a hyphenated word; it should be *oversight*.
4   A question mark is required after 'done'.
5   Some mark of punctuation is needed after 'taken'; a comma or
     preferably a dash to indicate emphasis.
6   *as* is quite unnecessary before *from*.
7   A hyphen is required between *check* and *system*.

Checking the figures carefully, the manager soon discovered the
cashier's mistake. Either an oversight or a wrong entry was responsible for the mistake. What was to be done? The manager was in a
quandary, but he felt that action had to be taken—and taken
quickly. He decided that from 1 March he would introduce a new
check-system.

Exercise six

1   There should be quotation marks before 'but' because direct
     speech continues.
2   *allusion* is used wrongly, the word should be *illusion*, meaning
     a false impression.
3   Managing Director should be preferred to managing director,
     because specific reference is being made to him.

4   *no body* must be written as one word, *nobody*.
5   There should be commas after 'nevertheless' and 'Brown' in order to isolate the parenthetical phrase *in fairness to Brown*.
6   A hyphen is required between *self* and *opinionated*.
7   *to be* should be *to have been* (the past infinitive) in order to maintain the tense sequence.
8   *uninterested* is used wrongly; it should be *disinterested*, meaning impartial, without self-interest.

'All right', he said, 'but I cannot agree with you. Brown seems to be under the illusion that the Managing Director was biased. I am sure that nobody else thought so. Nevertheless, in fairness to Brown, I must say that the Managing Director was somewhat self-opinionated in his remarks, and I should have preferred him to have been a little more disinterested.'

6 Style: guidelines and pitfalls

Vigorous writing is concise. A sentence should contain no unnecessary words, a paragraph no unnecessary sentences, for the same reason that a drawing should have no unnecessary lines and a machine no unnecessary parts. This requires not that the writer make all his sentences short, or that he avoid all detail and treat his subjects only in outline, but that every word should tell.

Professor William Strunk, Professor of English at Cornell University lectured this truth to his students in 1919. It still holds good today.

Omit needless words was one of his basic principles in the writing of English. We would do well to follow his advice and write: 'because' instead of 'in view of the fact that', 'whether' instead of 'the question as to whether', 'except' for 'with the exception of', 'decide' for 'arrive at a decision', and a host more unnecessary words. Let this, then, be a start to improving style—discarding needless words.

When we look at what we write, what do we see? Spelling mistakes galore; words constantly misused; frequent use of jargon; participles dangling everywhere; plural words with singular verbs; punctuation peppering our letters or leaving them all but barren.

Style in writing *is* important. What is style? Essentially, **style** is suitability; the suitability of words to the subject or the occasion. Here, the subject is *business*.

There is no special language for business, although some textbooks have encouraged the idea that business calls for some kind of separate language. This is no longer the case. Take one simple and obvious example: in business we do not 'describe', therefore the extensive use of adjectives is out of place. The fundamental considerations when writing business letters should be the three C's—*clarity, conciseness, courtesy*. To help you achieve the three C's, follow these guidelines:

Be accurate   The information you give in a business letter must be accurate. Make sure, therefore, that any facts and figures given are correct.

Think clearly   Think before you write so that the meaning conveyed in your letter will be clear, both to yourself and to the recipient.

Write simply   This should follow naturally from clear thinking, but too often complexities arise from the written word, and generally this stems from an artificial style. Get into the habit of using short words, short sentences, and short paragraphs; this makes a letter easy and quick to read. It will also be easier to understand.

Be brief   This means that you should use words economically; it does not mean that you have to be abrupt. In business no-one wants to read irrelevant or superfluous matter, for this is a waste of time.

Be positive   This does not mean being dogmatic; it simply means that you should have a positive rather than a negative approach. This adds clarity and point to your letter. Prefer the familiar word to the unfamiliar.

Be courteous   It is important in your letters to maintain a courteous manner. Business may very easily be lost on account of a rude or untidy letter. The firm or company to which you are writing will form its opinion of your firm or company by judging not only the facts of your letter but also its general tone. Try reading your letter aloud. Does it *sound* pleasant?

What of pitfalls? What, in fact, are you to guard against? Here are some of the more common pitfalls you should avoid.

Ambiguity

The dictionary tells us that this means double meaning, expression capable of more than one meaning. These examples help to illustrate this:

- Sandra told Linda that her mother was ill.

Ask yourself: who is ill? Is it Sandra's mother or Linda's?

- The manageress said to her assistant that the fault was hers.

Whose fault was it? Was it the fault of the manageress or of her assistant?

- The typewriter needed to be repaired badly.

'Badly' is, of course, out of place; the sentence should read:

- The typewriter badly needed to be repaired.

Ambiguity often arises from the use of involved and over-long sentences, phrases or words misplaced, and weak punctuation. Clear thinking before writing, therefore, is essential.

Cliché

A cliché is a hackneyed phrase or expression. The constant use of clichés produces staleness in both speech and writing, so avoid using them. Here are some examples:

- be that as it may; in well-informed circles; conspicuous by its absence; far be it from me to; at the parting of the ways; the psychological moment; leave no stone unturned; in any shape or form; last but not least; shrewd suspicion; it stands to reason; strange as it may seem; needless to say; no shadow of doubt

Colloquialism

This is the use of words, phrases or expressions acceptable in familiar or popular speech, but which are not suitable in formal speech or writing. Some examples are:

- quite all right; to go all out; couldn't care less; haven't a clue

The colloquial forms she'd, don't, he'll, I'll, etc., although used in ordinary conversation, are not used in formal writing except in direct quotation or dialogue.

Colloquialisms are not necessarily always bad English, but in a business letter they give the impression of slackness or laziness—and this is discourteous.

Slang

These are words, expressions, phrases in common colloquial use, but unacceptable in standard English. In another sense, they are a specialised vocabulary used by a class or group of people, by a trade, or by a profession. For example: a schoolboy talks of swotting, cribbing, a grind, prep.

Many expressions of slang have found their way into familiar speech. Here are a few:

- tight as a drum; to go off the deep-end; to give the OK; to get a kick out of; to tick off; scram; fed-up with; browned off

You should be on constant guard against introducing any slang into business letters, for it both cheapens and weakens your writing.

Redundancy

This is the use of unnecessary words. For example:

- The shop assistant restored the umbrella back to its owner.

Restored means gave back, so the same thing is being said twice.

Therefore the word back is redundant and should be omitted:
- The shop assistant restored the umbrella to its owner.
- She was often in the habit of going to the cinema.

Here the word often means the same as in the habit of and is therefore redundant. The sentence should read:
- She was in the habit of going to the cinema.

Commercial jargon

The fact that there is no special language for business has already been emphasised. Modern business practice has happily done away with the ponderous and stilted expression so common only a few years ago. Writing for business today calls primarily for clarity, conciseness, and brevity. The old-fashioned phrase 'We beg to acknowledge receipt of' has at last died, replaced by the simple 'Thank you for your letter' or 'We have received your letter'.

Commercial jargon, sometimes called officialese, is not always easy to recognise, for it is an insidious disease that creeps into letters, no matter how careful you are. Its main symptoms are: circumlocution (the use of many words where few would do); the use of long words for short words; unfamiliar words for familiar; phrases for single words; padding (filling-out with unnecessary words); the flush of new words and phrases.

Here are listed some of the words, phrases, and expressions you should avoid. Beside each is a simple and straightforward translation for use in your letters. These are only a few; there are many more.

It has been brought to our notice	We note. We notice
I am wholly at a loss to understand	I cannot understand
It will be our earnest endeavour	We shall try
Enclosed please find.	
We enclose herewith	We enclose
We are of the opinion that	We think that
your good selves	you
in spite of the fact that	although
at your earliest convenience	as soon as possible
I have instituted the necessary enquiries	I am enquiring
downward movement in prices	fall in prices
It is within our power	We can
We are prepared to offer	We offer. We can offer
Your order to hand	We have received your order
It is incumbent upon you	You must

Omit from your vocabulary we beg to remain; do not use commence when you mean begin, advise when you mean inform, acquire for get or obtain, purchase for buy. Communication is a long way of saying letter or inquiry. Send is so much simpler than dispatch, and anticipate is too often used when you simply mean expect. At all costs, avoid using the ridiculous word same in your letters. For example:

- We have received your order for two lawnmowers, and shall send same by rail tomorrow.

This awkward word simply means the matter or the problem or your inquiry or it or them, depending on what it is you are referring to. Write instead:

- We have received your order for two lawnmowers, and shall send *them* by rail tomorrow.

Always try to use the simplest word and so give your letter a business-like clarity. Beware of using new jargon; beware the cult of *wise*—tax*wise* and price*wise*, weather*wise* and road*wise*. As with the old, keep new jargon out of your letters.

Finally, whenever you want to use any of these words—instance, case, character, condition, state, circumstance, degree, nature—stop and think. Ask yourself: What am I trying to say? Then say it, clearly and concisely, avoiding such woolly words.

Exercise

Re-write these sentences in concise and clear English, giving reasons for your corrections. In a few of the examples you may have to recast the sentence.

1   The one is equally as bad as the other.

2   The boss went off the deep end when I told him.

3   We are instituting many meaningful changes in the curriculum.

4   He said to Ahmad that the responsibility was his.

5   We learn from well-informed circles that now is the psychological moment to show just where we stand; now is the time when no stone must be left unturned if we are to achieve our target.

6   You must come to a final decision.

7   There is no shadow of doubt that the salesgirl is lying.

8   It was clearly obvious that he couldn't care less.

9   It will be our earnest endeavour to execute your order at the very earliest opportunity.

10 If your goodselves will furnish the necessary particulars from the catalogue enclosed herewith, we will be pleased to execute your order.

11 Without exception we decided unanimously to adopt the proposal.

12 Fishwise this restaurant is excellent.

13 Those who had been so anxious to call the meeting were, when it came to the crunch, conspicuous by their absence.

14 The reason why the estimate was low was because they were anxious to land the contract.

15 In the light of experience it is my opinion that the escalation of prices will continue for some considerable time.

16 It would appear that, in the foreseeable future, there is little or no hope of a reasoned settlement.

17 He sent in his notice because he was browned-off with the office set-up.

18 It's OK by me.

19 It is high time we arrived at a decision as to whether or not we should up-grade our prices.

20 I am inclined to the view that, under existing circumstances, there is, prima facie, a case for expansion of our firm.

7 Planning a business letter

In all writing we write to be understood; this is particularly important in the writing of business letters. It should be easier to write a clear and concise letter than an essay or a report because in letter-writing the reader is easily visualised. This is worth remembering.

A letter has two purposes. It is both a messenger and an ambassador. As a messenger it carries what you want to say to its recipient; as an ambassador it carries your image, the image of the firm or organisation or association for which you work. Therefore, if you are to write a good business letter, you must be clearly understood and you must create the right impression, both in content and presentation.

Chapter 6 listed six guidelines to style: *be accurate*; *think clearly*; *write simply*; *be brief*; *be positive*; *be courteous*. To these add *the rule of the five questions*—questions you have to ask yourself as you write your letters.

Question one *What are you to say?* This simply means that you have to think clearly and concisely before you write; you have to be sure in your own mind what you want to say. If you are not clear on this point, how can you expect the recipient of your letter to grasp what you have written?

If you have several items you want to write about, why not list them? This can help.

Question two *Are you being logical?* Are you jumping from one point to another with no reason or order? Your aim must be to take points in a logical sequence so that, to both you and its reader, your letter has ordered content and meaning.

Question three *What about your paragraphs?* You have decided what to say; you have arranged your thoughts. Now, think about paragraphs. Remember that a letter without paragraphs can be both confusing to read and difficult to grasp. Paragraphs are signposts to the reader that you have finished with one point and are moving on to the next. Use your paragraphs, therefore, as signposts.

Your letter may be complex. If so, you should give each paragraph a heading, each pointing the way. The paragraph should be kept short, however. If it has to be long, break it down into sub-paragraphs. Also, in a business letter, consider using numbers to emphasise the content of the paragraphs.

Question four *Have you identified the subject?* In other words, does the reader know what your letter is about? It is sometimes useful to give the letter itself a heading; this immediately identifies the subject.

Question five *Have you shown the way ahead?* Your letter should end by signposting the way ahead, so that both you and the reader clearly understand what is to happen next.

Remember then, as you write your letters, to ask yourself these five questions—what are you to say; are you being logical; what about your paragraphs; have you identified the subject; have you shown the way ahead? Learn to produce letters that are neatly set out and well-presented, free from errors and jargon. In this way you create a favourable image for your firm. A poor letter, no matter how important its content, only irritates and does nothing to help a firm's business. Therefore, cherish this as your golden rule—*Never let a letter go without being satisfied with it.*

Study this letter. Does it follow the guidelines mentioned?
Yes—for it is accurate and clear; it is simple and brief; it is positive
and courteous. Therefore it gives a good image of you and your firm.

PLASTICHROME & CO LTD

Directors:
H Morton
J A Blakey
T Y Thomson

Tel: 0902-3468/9
Highfield Works
Wolverhampton WV6 8DW

Your Ref SD 181   1 September 19..
Our Ref   JW/EB

The Chief Buyer
Stone & Goldie Ltd
21 Bridge Street
Manchester M14 4P6

Dear Sir

We have pleasure in enclosing our receipt
for your cheque of £36.

You were quite right to deduct the
discount of ten per cent, according to
the special arrangements made with you
when the order was placed.

Thank you for your order received today.
The goods will be sent in about ten days'
time.

                    Yours faithfully

                    John H Wright
                    (Sales Manager)

Look at this one. It is a straightforward inquiry about a hotel booking.

Tel: Wideopen 3871

10 Pennington Avenue
Grays Park
Newcastle upon Tyne
NE5 9QH
25 February 19..

The Booking Clerk
Manor Hotel
Duns, Berwickshire
Scotland

Dear Sir

I write to ask if you can offer the following accommodation:
(a) comfortable twin-bedded room for Mr & Mrs R Paterson
(b) comfortable twin-bedded room for Mr & Mrs W F Mavor
for 18 and 19 May inclusive, both with private bathrooms.

The four of us would arrive mid-morning on Friday 18 May and leave after lunch on Sunday 20 May.

I understand that your charge for bed and breakfast is £30.50 per double room. Perhaps you would confirm this. It would be helpful also to know your charge for dinner.

I hope you can accommodate us.

Yours faithfully
Ferrier Mavor
(W F Mavor)

The inquiry brought this reply:

Manor Hotel
Duns, Berwickshire
Tel: 03612-231

Our ref   DAH/JA/1

2 March 19..

Mr W F Mavor
10 Pennington Avenue
Grays Park
Newcastle upon Tyne
NE5 9QH

Dear Mr Mavor

Thank you for your letter of 25 February.

I can offer the accommodation you require,
and have provisionally reserved two twin-
bedded rooms with private bathrooms for
the nights of 18 and 19 May.

The charge for double room and breakfast
is £31.25, inclusive of service charge,
plus VAT. Dinner is £6.50 per person.

Please let me know if this booking is
acceptable. I enclose a brochure about
the hotel.

Yours sincerely

D A Hogarth
Booking Clerk

Enc

It is both a messenger and an ambassador. It answers the questions asked in a positive and courteous way. Each paragraph leads logically to the next. The final paragraph is the signpost ahead—the recipient now has to reply.

Note that the letter is typed in fully blocked and open punctuated form (see page 76).

Now look at this letter:

```
Dear Sirs

Thank you for your letter of 18 February
in which you advise us that the tools
ordered by you on 4 January have not been
received by you. On receipt of your letter
we at once looked into this matter and
found that your order was despatched to
your Branch Office in Islington instead
of to your Main Factory.

We are sending a further delivery as per
your original order by British Rail to
reach you no later than next Monday.
Please telephone me on receipt so that
I will know that delivery has been made.

I have telephoned your manager at the Main
Factory and explained the position to him,
asking him to return the original delivery
to us.

Yours faithfully
```

This letter is not much of a messenger and less of an ambassador. There is too much commercial jargon in it—'advise us'; 'on receipt of'; 'further delivery as per'—too much repetition of expression and, worst of all, there is no apology for an obvious mistake by the despatch department.

Here is an improved version:

```
Dear Sirs

Thank you for your letter of 18 February.

Due to a mistake in our despatch depart-
ment the tools you ordered on 4 January
were sent to your Branch Office at
Islington instead of to your Main Factory.

We have today sent a replacement delivery
by British Rail; this should reach you by
next Monday. Perhaps you would telephone
me when it arrives so that I know you have
received it.

We do regret this mistake and the incon-
venience caused you.

Yours faithfully
```

Why is this version better than the original? It is free from jargon; its language is simple and positive; the mistake is directly acknowledged and put right at once; apology is made. By such a reply you have restored the relationship between your firm and the order firm.

Here is another set of letters to study. The first is a letter of inquiry.

Hotel Excelsior

Bukit Nanas   *Tel:* 926890/926891
Kuala Lumpur 01.02   *Telex:* Excel 3486

Sales Manager   27 June 19..
Choong Carpets Ltd
22/24 Sin Tong Industrial Estate
Singapore 20

Dear Sir

We are considering re-carpeting all
bedrooms, staircases, and corridors on
5th and 6th floors of our hotel. We
estimate that we shall require approximately 4680 m^2.

Would you please provide information on
the types and quality of carpeting you
have available, together with the range
of prices. It would be helpful if you
would also let us know what arrangements
you would be able to make to carry out
this work.

We look forward to an early reply.

                    Yours faithfully

                    J R Rajasooria
                    (Purchase Manager)

This is a straightforward, direct inquiry, set down in simple
language, listing specific information, and asking specific questions.

Now look at the second letter—the reply to the inquiry letter.

Choong Carpets Ltd

22/24 Sin Tong Industrial Estate
Singapore 20
Tel: 4534681/2

Mr J R Rajasooria   6 July 19..
Purchase Manager
Hotel Excelsior
Bukit Nanas
Kuala Lumpur 01.02

Dear Sir

With reference to your esteemed enquiry of
27 June, I am pleased to send you the
information you require.

We can provide two qualities of carpeting,
namely Special grade suitable for bedrooms
- if the intention is to provide luxury
with endurance, and Plus grade for
corridors and staircases where primary
importance is long wear, both of which
are available in a wide range of self-
colours and patterns, with a three year
guarantee against fading.

Enclosed please find our catalogue, and
note that there are reduced prices for
bulk purchase.

You will appreciate that underfelt will
be required and we take the opportunity
of enclosing samples of same for your
examination.

Prices quoted in the catalogue do not
include laying which would be the subject
of a separate estimate by our carpet
layers.

We have arranged for our representative
to call on your goodselves to assist you
in the selection of the most suitable
grades, taking all circumstances into
consideration.

Yours faithfully

Lok Yee Wong
Sales Manager

You do not have to read this letter a second time to recognise its defects. Firstly, look at it in a general way. It is far too long-winded and woolly to be in any way a satisfactory reply to a letter of inquiry, and the gigantic second sentence is especially difficult to digest. There is no crispness: it lacks clarity and even courtesy. In fact, it seems to take for granted that Mr Rajasooria, Purchase Manager of Hotel Excelsior, is going to place the order with Choong Carpets Ltd.

Secondly, it is overloaded with business jargon, outmoded words and expressions, verbosity, and circumlocution. Here are some examples: 'with reference to your esteemed enquiry'; 'your good-selves'; 'taking all circumstances into consideration'.

In addition there is no typed reference to 'Encs'.

All in all, this letter is no messenger, certainly no ambassador.

Now look at the letter on page 70. Here the reply is quite different from the letter above. It is crisp, clear, and concise. It answers the questions of the first letter in a way that leaves no room for doubt. It indicates what is available; it signposts ahead; it is economical with words without being abrupt. It follows the guidelines of a good business letter. It is both a messenger and an ambassador. Study it carefully. It is, of course, not the only type of business letter that could have been sent, but it will serve as a sound model for your practice in writing business letters.

Dear Sir

Thank you for enquiry of 27 June about carpeting. In reply, I hope this information will be useful.

We stock two grades of carpeting suitable for your purpose.

1. Special Grade: combines luxury with durability; very suitable for bedrooms.

2. Plus Grade: long wearing; of good quality; recommended for corridors and stairs.

Both grades are available in a wide range of self-colours and patterns; both carry a three year guarantee against fading.

I enclose our catalogue; the reduced prices quoted are for bulk purchase. Samples of underfelt are also enclosed, with prices listed.

The carpet prices quoted do not include the charge for laying. This can be estimated separately by our carpet layers.

If you are interested, I shall be pleased to arrange for our representative to see you. This can be arranged easily and quickly. We look forward to hearing from you.

Yours faithfully

Lok Yee Wong
Sales Manager

Encs

8 Lay-out of a business letter

Letter head

First of all comes the letter head. This is a sheet of letter paper with a printed heading carrying the firm's name, address, telephone number(s) and telex number (if there is one), name of manager, directors, etc. These are a few examples:

Lowland Malt Distillers Limited

Directors: T M Smith (Chairman) W V Hannah, J K R Black

Export Department

Telephone 041-258 4018
Telegrams Madis Glasgow
Telex Madis 7349

68 Waterloo Street
Glasgow G5 6PW

FAX MERCHANDISING

68 Campbell Street
YABA – LAGOS

Tel: Lagos 54569
Cable: FAXLA

Carfax National Building Society

12 Prince Street, Edinburgh EH2 1JB Tel: 031-661 2417
General Manager T S Mead FCIS

Your Ref

Our Ref

Note, however, that there is no absolute form for a letter head. It can take different forms, depending on what information is to be conveyed and on a firm's practice and choice of design.

Lay-out

This covers the following:

1	Date	6	Body of letter
2	Reference(s)	7	Complimentary ending
3	Inside address	8	Signature and conclusion
4	Salutation	9	Enclosure(s)
5	Subject-heading		

Framework

The framework of a letter is set out opposite. Here are details of its contents:

1   Date   This should be written in full, normally in the order of day, month, year, as in:

- 15 November 19..

Commas should be omitted. The day of the week is not generally included, but if it is, it should be shown on a separate line. The appearance is then better if the year is moved to a line of its own, e.g.

- Tuesday
  15 November
  19..

2   Reference(s)   References are a way of identifying a letter. They vary from the very simple to the complex. In basic form they are the initials of the person who dictated the letter and the typist, e.g.

- Our ref: WFM/OP

Sometimes a file number is added, as in:

- WFM/OP/69

More complex references may relate to filing/systems or to an account number or to a client's number, e.g.

- WFM/OP/69/8

This could mean that this particular letter is the eighth written in subject file 69.

There are two points to remember when using references:

a be sure that your own references give the necessary information for locating the letter at a later date

b in reply, always quote the other party's letter reference

BOON & LEE LTD   Building Contractors

78–80 Still Road   Branch Manager
Singapore 15   R A Lim
Tel: 041–3326   Telex: Habo 5821

2 ....   1 ....

3 ....
....
....

4 ....

5 ....

6 ....
....
....
....
....
....
....
....
....
....

7 ....
....

8 ....

9 ....

The key to this framework is on pages 72 to 77.

3 Inside address   This is the name and address of the person to whom the letter is being sent. It may be in **block** form, as in:

- The Manager
  Fax Merchandising
  68 Campbell Street
  YABA—LAGOS

or in **indented** form, as in:

- The Manager
     Fax Merchandising
        68 Campbell Street
          YABA—LAGOS

The block form is to be preferred.

If possible, the address should be confined to three or four lines. If necessary the name of a town and county may be included in one line, e.g.

- The Secretary
  Nu-Lino Company
  41 King Street
  Preston, Lancs

Note carefully the use of **Messrs**. It should be used when addressing a partnership, as in:

- Messrs Smith & Moodie; Messrs W Black & Company

Note, however, that Messrs should not be used when writing to a limited company; your letter should be addressed to The Secretary or to some other official of the company, e.g. General Manager, Manager, Accountant, etc. For example:

- The Secretary   The Sales Manager
  Smith and Webb Ltd   O P Martin & Co Ltd

Note also that Messrs should *not* be used:

a where the name of a firm contains a conferred title, e.g.

- Sir John Wilson & Sons Ltd

b where the name is preceded by the word 'The', e.g.

- The Mike Jones Shoe Company

c where the name of the firm contains no personal names, e.g.

- New Furnishings Co

Letters for the attention of   Practice here varies, but you should keep to the formal procedure and set out your letter like this:

- Smith & Jones Ltd
  14 High Street
  Carlisle

  For the attention of Mr Thomas

  Dear Mr Thomas

A particular letter may be confidential; when this is so, the word 'Confidential' should be typed above the address in the letter and in the top left-hand corner of the envelope.

4 Salutation The normal form of salutation in business correspondence is:

● Dear Sir(s) or Dear Madam (Mesdames)

Two further forms of salutation must be considered:

a *Sir, Gentlemen, Madam, Mesdames*. These are used in more formal correspondence, namely, official reports and government correspondence, etc.

b *Dear Mr (Mrs/Miss/Ms), Dear* . . . This form permits the only use of 'Yours sincerely' in business letters and is used only when the person addressed is known by the writer. Firms may have their own rules about this practice.

There are, of course, special forms of address, e.g. to nobility, to the clergy, etc. These are listed in any good dictionary.

5 Subject heading In business letters this is used to give prominence to the subject matter, as in this example:

● Dear Sir,
  Mr H J Stewart

  This young man has applied to us for a post in our Advertising Department. He states that . . .

The subject heading should be underlined.

6 Body of letter This is obviously the most important section of any business letter. The basic guidelines are: use concise and clear English; uncomplicated words; accurate spelling; considered punctuation; sensible paragraphing. Beware of too many short paragraphs since these tend to spoil the appearance of a letter. Note also that a letter, unless very short, should never be written in one paragraph.

Avoid the use of abbreviations other than accepted ones. Be careful when using the ampersand (&) for 'and'; it should not be used in the body of the letter except:

a in reference to a firm, e.g. Brown & Company
b when referring to numbers, e.g. pages 6 & 8

Most firms now use the fully blocked, open punctuation form of letter. There are two reasons for this: firstly, many consider it improves the appearance of a letter; secondly—and more importantly—it saves much typewriting time.

Most of the letters in the next chapter are fully blocked and have open punctuation. The easiest way for you to understand what is meant by the term is to take a look at the examples of different kinds of business letters in Chapter 9. Look at the letter on page 78, for instance.

Fully blocked describes the shape of paragraphs which are blocked from the left-hand margin rather than indented in the first line. When a paragraph ends we move down two line spaces and begin again at the left-hand margin.

Open punctuation means the complete omission of all punctuation for the date, inside address, salutation, complimentary close etc. without risking ambiguity. Naturally, punctuation is retained for the body of the letter. Given a clear-cut typeface and even block typing with adequate white space between paragraphs so that eye and mind are not confused, the fully blocked, open punctuated style is both attractive and economical.

7 Complimentary ending   The point to remember here is that your ending must conform with your salutation. Here are some examples:

- Dear Sir/Madam   :   Yours faithfully

   Dear Mr Paignton
   Dear Mrs Wilson   :   Yours sincerely
   Dear Oscar

Yours truly or Yours very truly is sometimes used in place of Yours sincerely, when the relationship may not be so personal, but this practice has largely disappeared. Its use is not recommended. The use of 'I remain' before the ending is outmoded and should be forgotten.

Note the more formal endings:

- Sir/Gentlemen   :   Your obedient servant
   Madam/Mesdames   :   Yours respectfully

These are rarely used.

8 Signature and conclusion   The name of the firm or position held is normally typed immediately below the complimentary ending, allowing sufficient space for signature. Many signatures to business letters are illegible; when this is so, a sensible practice is to type the name under the signature.

If the firm's title is used, whether written, typed or rubber-stamped, the person signing should add his initials.

Here are some examples of formal signatures:

- Sole trader : Michael Brown
  Partnership : May Banks & Co
  Limited company : For King, Miles & Co Ltd,
  Peter Long
  Director
  Local authority : Newcastle Urban District Council
  Roger Caird
  Clerk to the Council

Each member of a partnership signs in the style adopted by the firm, for example:

- Joseph Banks
  Partner

In the case of a limited company the official who signs may be the Director, Accountant, Secretary, Sales Manager, or other official concerned with the matter in question.

Per pro or pp is an abbreviation for the Latin per procurationem, indicating that the signatory has signed for and on behalf of the company with full authority. Persons who are authorised to conduct correspondence for their firm, but who have not been given power of procuration, sign as follows:

- R Baird
  pp May Banks & Co

9 Enclosure(s) These are shown by the abbreviation Enc or Encs (if more than one), entered at the bottom left-hand margin. There are other ways of indicating enclosures:

a by a stick-on enclosure slip on which is written the number of enclosures

b by a solidus (/) typed in the margin opposite the reference to the enclosure in the letter itself

c by three dashes (- - -) typed in the margin opposite the reference to the enclosure in the letter

These, then, are the component parts of a business letter. There may be some variations to the above framework, but they will be only slight. Remember what was said in Chapter 7—your letter has to be both a messenger and an ambassador. Therefore, excellence in letter-writing becomes an essential.

Let us now look at various types of business letter.

9 Different types of business letter

Quotations

The first step in a business transaction is usually an inquiry about prices, range of goods, availability of goods, etc. In order to discover new sources of supply or to obtain details of quality and price the buyer sends inquiries to several firms.

Thomson & Son Limited

16 Gordon Street   *Tel:* 041/334/6913
Glasgow G2 9GH

Ref   JK/RS

1 March 19..

The Manager
Border Tweeds Ltd
Kelso
Roxburghshire

Dear Sir

We are interested in tweed lengths suitable for skirt-making and would like to
have details of your prices and terms.

It would be helpful if you could supply
samples.

Yours faithfully

James Kerr
Chief Buyer

He will receive in return a quotation.

Border Tweeds Ltd

Kelso
Roxburghshire
Tel: 05732-268

Your ref   JK/RS   6 March 19..
Our ref   RT/IM

Mr J Kerr
Chief Buyer
Thomson & Son Ltd
16 Gordon Street
Glasgow G2 9GH

Dear Mr Kerr

Thank you for your inquiry of 1 March.

We can supply the following tweed lengths
from stock:

Shade No 32 in 40 m lengths @ £3.15 per m
Shade No 38 in 30 m lengths @ £3.75 per m
Shade No 47 in 30 m lengths @ £4.50 per m
Shade No 58 in 60 m lengths @ £6.00 per m

All are suitable for skirt-making; samples
of each are enclosed.

Terms are 5% discount (7 days), $2\frac{1}{2}$% (30
days), carriage forward.

We hope you will place an order with us.

                    Yours sincerely

                    Ron Turner
                    (Manager)

Encs

When submitting a quotation, the following points should be noted:

1 A clear description of the goods offered should be given. Where possible, samples should be sent.
2 Prices and terms should be given. Discounts, if any, should be shown.
3 Delivery terms should be stated, e.g. carriage paid or carriage forward.
4 If there is a limiting period, then this should be indicated, e.g. subject to acceptance within 14 days.

Order letters

When ordering goods, care must be taken to state requirements clearly so that the seller will not be confused about the exact goods asked for. It should never be necessary for him to refer to former orders or to write for further details. If goods are ordered from a catalogue or numbered list, the clearest indication that can be given is to quote the catalogue or list number.

The date when delivery is required should be stated, also the preferred method of transport—road, rail, sea, or air. The goods may be required at the office address or at the warehouse address of the firm; they may even be delivered direct to the address of a customer of the buyers. It is essential, therefore, to state where the goods are to be sent.

Remember that all relevant information should be given in an order letter. It is more business-like—and certainly it helps to prevent orders being misread—to tabulate the items required.

As a guide to the paragraphing of an order letter you should include:

a reference to a source of information
b list of goods to be ordered
c quantity, quality, price, catalogue number (if any)
d details of delivery and payment
e an order number

An example of a firm's order letter with good paragraphing is shown opposite.

Thomson & Son Limited

16 Gordon Street   *Tel:* 041/334/6913
Glasgow G2 9GH

Ref   JK/RS

10 March 19..

Mr R Turner
Manager
Border Tweeds Ltd
Kelso
Roxburghshire

Dear Mr Turner

Thank you for your quotation of 6 March,
also for the samples of tweed.

Please will you forward the following
lengths:

6 - 40 m lengths tweed, Shade No 32
                            £3.15 per m
3 - 30 m lengths tweed, Shade No 47
                            £4.50 per m
3 - 60 m lengths tweed, Shade No 58
                            £6.00 per m

by British Road Services to the above
address, order no 68.

Your terms are acceptable. Please deliver
by 25 March as the tweed is required to
complete an urgent export order.

Yours sincerely

James Kerr
Chief Buyer

Alternatively, the order may be written on an order form and enclosed with a short letter as follows:

Thomson & Son Limited

16 Gordon Street   *Tel:* 041/334/6913
Glasgow G2 9GH

Ref   JK/RS

10 March 19..

Mr R Turner
Manager
Border Tweeds Ltd
Kelso
Roxburghshire

Dear Mr Turner

Thank you for your quotation of 6 March,
also for the samples of tweed.

We enclose our order no 68 to be sent by
British Road Services. Please deliver by
25 March as the tweed is required to
complete an urgent export order.

Yours sincerely

James Kerr
Chief Buyer

Enc

Acknowledgments

Often, orders will be placed by telephone or telex, but they will always be acknowledged by letter. Acknowledgments should include thanks for the order; confirmation of details; delivery date; courtesy ending.

Here is an example of an acknowledgment by letter:

Jackson & Co Inc

856 Third Avenue
New York NY 10022
Tel: 212-224-6968

WM/MT

June 13 19..

Mr G Grainger
Purchasing Officer
Smart & Sons Ltd
160 Crow Road
Don Mills
Ontario
Canada

Dear Mr Grainger

Thank you for your order no 248 of 10 June
for linen and silks. We have the goods in
stock and shall send them tomorrow by
rail.

You should therefore receive them within
seven days.

Yours sincerely

W P Martin
(Textiles Manager)

Note: Modern practice in business is to reduce as many letters as possible to standard forms, particularly orders and acknowledgments. Many small firms, however, still order and acknowledge by letter.

Exercise

Write appropriate letters from these notes:

1 Porteous Bros PO Box 1349, Accra, Ghana order the following goods from Meyrick & Co, 16 George Lane, Tayton, Leeds L3:
    150 litres lead paint, col grey, cat no 613
    60 litres creosote (standard)
Delivery is to be made by 20 March by sea and road.

2 Meyrick & Co acknowledge the order, promising delivery as requested.

3 Heralds & Co, St Peter Port, Jersey, Channel Isles, have received prices and patterns of carpets from Lord & Co, Wolverhampton, WV2 3HQ. They place this order:
    12 Wilton carpets, size 4 m × 3 m, colour no 3
    12 Axminster carpets, size 4 m × 3½ m, colour no 7
to be sent by road transport and by sea, fob. Delivery date: within one month.

4 Jones & Co, 4 Grange Street, Newcastle upon Tyne, NE2 3TL, order a consignment of fruit from Noyes & Porter, 56 Weald Road, London E17 5LE. The fruit is to be sent by the Midlands Express Carrier Co, and is required by the end of the week. Noyes & Porter find that one item ordered cannot be forwarded as requested, as a shipment of that kind of fruit is not due until Saturday. Delivery of the other items is promised by the end of the week, and particulars are given regarding the completion of the order.
    Write the letter ordering the fruit, and the acknowledgment.

5 Ban Cheong & Co, 168 Prangin Way, Penang send an order to Lim Kuang Plastics, 7D Lokyang Park, Jurong, Singapore 22 for:
    200 Plastic Containers no 8 as shown on p 4 of list
    360 Plastic Trays no 12 as shown on p 6 of list
to be sent by rail, delivery not later than 15 days.
    Write the letter ordering the goods, and the reply.

6 The Sales Manager of your firm—an office equipment firm—is to visit the United Arab Emirates on business. He plans to stay one week; he will require secretarial services. Write to: Holiday Inn, PO Box 5802, Sharjah, United Arab Emirates, making a provisional reservation pending reply to your inquiry. Include your firm's letter head.

Letters of complaint

It is sometimes necessary to make a complaint about the quality of goods received or about damage which has occurred before the goods reach the buyer's premises. Late or incomplete delivery might also cause dissatisfaction. Whatever the reason for complaint, annoyance must never be allowed to take precedence over courtesy.

Here is an example of a letter complaining about delay in delivery:

Hunt & Son

14 Percy Street
Penzance PZ6 05Q   Tel: 0632-88689

PB/ST

4 June 19..

The Manager
Steel Cables Ltd
60 Alton Street
Coventry CV3 6NT

Dear Sir

On 15 May we ordered from you a consignment of steel cables for delivery by 31
May.

As we have not yet received the cables,
would you please look into the matter
and arrange their dispatch without
further delay?

Yours faithfully

Peter Bryce
Warehouse Manager

It should always be remembered that the sender of goods may not be responsible for the condition about which complaint is made. Damage to the goods may be the fault of the carriers and not of the packing; delay in delivery may be traceable to the same cause or to a mistake in ordering. Delivery of insufficient goods or of goods not required may be the result of the buyer's carelessness in verifying the details of the order.

The following points should be embodied in a letter of complaint:

a delivery of goods should be acknowledged
b cause for complaint should be stated
c request for action should be made
d if necessary, replacement of goods should be asked for

The following is an example of a letter complaining about damaged goods.

---

                                        19 Mentone Terrace
                                        Edinburgh EH9 1LY
                                        9 January 19..

The Condé Publications Ltd
4 Bellevue Road
London SW5

Dear Sirs

As a regular subscriber to your magazine
'Good Food', I was most disappointed to
receive my January copy in such poor
condition. The cover was torn and adrift
from the magazine which had obviously
been packed with no backing.

I shall be glad to receive a replacement,
and hope that you will ensure that future
copies sent to me will be suitably packed.

                        Yours faithfully

                        Fraser Morton

A stronger, more decisive tone may be adopted if there has been a previous cause for complaint, but discourtesy is unnecessary and should be avoided. The following letter illustrates the point.

Jackson & Co Inc

856 Third Avenue
New York NY 10022
Tel: 212-224-6968

AW/IP/105   May 3 19..

Sales Manager
Henderson Bros
400 Fremont
San Francisco
CA 94105

Dear Sir

The three bales of silk of our order
N.369 of 2 April arrived today.

On examination we find them soiled at the
edges because of torn outer wrappings.
This is not the first time that we have
had to make such a complaint about cloth
received from you, and we must ask you to
see that goods sent to us are more
carefully packed.

The bales of silk are usable, but we feel
that you should allow us a reduction of
20 per cent on the price. The bales are
available for inspection should you wish
to appoint a representative.

              Yours faithfully

              Arthur White
              Purchasing Manager

Replies to complaints

In replying to a complaint about damaged goods, delay in delivery, etc., the seller should first of all express regret that the need for complaint has arisen. He should state what investigations have been made, and where the blame appears to lie. If the buyer is responsible, then it is wise to admit this frankly. Finally, the seller must suggest a remedy for the complaint—delayed goods must be forwarded, damaged goods must be replaced, etc.

Here are replies to two of the letters of complaint:

The Condé Publications Ltd

4 Bellevue Road
London SW5

14 January 19..

Fraser Morton Esq
19 Mentone Terrace
Edinburgh EH9 1LY

Dear Mr Morton

Thank you for your letter of 9 January.
I was sorry to learn that you received
your copy of 'Good Food' in such poor
condition.

I have now arranged to send a replacement
copy properly packed, and have taken the
necessary steps to ensure that future copies will reach you in perfect condition.

Please accept our apology for the inconvenience caused.

Yours sincerely

Robert James
Business Manager

Steel Cables Ltd

60 Alton Street
Coventry CV3 6NT   Tel: 0203/86962

JT/SR

7 June 19..

Mr P Bryce
Warehouse Manager
Messrs Hunt & Son
14 Percy Street
Penzance PZ6 05Q

Dear Mr Bryce

Thank you for your letter of 4 June. We
regret the delay in delivery of the steel
cables ordered by you on 15 May.

A recent strike at the factory has held up
production. The dispute, however, has been
settled and we are now able to fulfil our
orders.

Your consignment has been sent today, and
we hope the delay has not seriously in-
convenienced you.

Yours sincerely

James Thorpe
(Home Sales Manager)

Exercise

Write suitable letters from the following notes:

1   *a* Seeley & Co, Beresford Lane, Swansea SW6 9LP write to Waters & Sons, 3 Crouch Corner, Sheffield S2 6BL, complaining of damage done to two mahogany cabinets received. They are returning the damaged goods, and ask for immediate replacements.

    b Waters & Sons promise to replace the cabinets at once, but disclaim responsibility for damage. They state that the railway authorities have been informed.

2   *a* On 1 July Carnie Bros, Peel Street, Southampton SO1 1QU ordered from Primmer & Leeds, 14 Sefton Place, London W6 the following goods:

        35 men's drip-dry shirts (assorted) no 24.

    These were to be delivered by 10 June. On 13 July the goods had not arrived, and Carnie Bros ask for information about them.

    b Primmer & Leeds have overlooked the order, owing to heavy pressure of business. They promise to send the goods immediately by Motor Express Co Ltd.

3   One tonne granulated sugar has been bought from Purdie & Sons, 15–17 Brough Street, London N2 by Davidson Bros, 3 Carter Street, Nottingham NG1 7GG. On arrival the sugar is found to be of inferior quality; it is also damp. Purdie & Sons agree to replace it, as it is part of a new consignment which they have received and sent out unexamined due to pressure of work.

    Write both the letter of complaint and the reply.

4   Arnold Thin & Co of Bread Lane, Nottingham NG7 2RT, have ordered the following books from Smart's Publishing House, 53 The Wynd, Derby D1 2GA:

    1   36 copies of *Electrical Who's Who*
    2   24 copies of *Electrical Resistance of Metals*
    3   6 copies of *The Electronic Trader*

On delivery, 4 copies of no 3 were missing. Payment is being withheld meantime.

Requests for payment

A first letter requesting payment of an account is generally very short. With it is enclosed the statement of account, and reference should be made to any terms of discount.

Garton Brothers
22 Baker Road
Huddersfield HD3 3EX
Tel: 0484/33631

24 May 19..

The Chief Accountant
Tilden & Sprott Ltd
3 Grange Lane
York
YO2 5DS

Dear Sir

We enclose statement of account for gaskets
ordered by you on 14 May. A discount of
3 per cent is allowed on accounts settled
within one month.

Yours faithfully

Mary Percy (Mrs)
Credit Controller

MP/MD/19

Enc

If settlement is not made as a result of this letter, a further letter in more personal language should be sent when the discount period has elapsed. It is as well to remember that payment may be due to an oversight or to unbusiness-like methods of dealing with accounts.

The customer should be reminded of the debt and of the fact that no discount can now be given. If there has been difficulty in obtaining the goods or in delivering them on the required date, or if a promise of payment by a certain date has not been kept, then it is advisable to bring these facts to the notice of the customer.

Garton Brothers

22 Baker Road
Huddersfield HD3 3EX
Tel: 0484/33631

24 June 19..

The Chief Accountant
Tilden & Sprott Ltd
3 Grange Lane
York
YO2 5DS

Dear Sir

We have to remind you that your account
for gaskets ordered on 14 May has not yet
been paid. Discount cannot now be allowed.

You will remember that we went to some
trouble to meet your delivery dates, and
we are sure that you would not wish to
inconvenience us by delaying payment.

A copy of the account is enclosed, and we
shall be glad to receive your cheque.

Yours faithfully

Mary Percy (Mrs)
Credit Controller

MP/MD/19

Enc

When the second request for payment does not bring settlement it is possible that the customer is purposely withholding it. The tone of the next letter should be curt and pointed, but still courteous.

Garton Brothers

22 Baker Road
Huddersfield HD3 3EX
Tel: 0484/33631

8 September 19..

The Chief Accountant
Tilden & Sprott Ltd
3 Grange Lane
York
YO2 5DS

Dear Sir

Enclosed is the account for goods
ordered on 14 May. This account is now
long overdue. We shall be glad to have
settlement without further delay.

Yours faithfully

Mary Percy (Mrs)
Credit Controller

MP/MD/19

Enc

If persuasion and curtness have not had the desired result, legal proceedings, as a last resort, are threatened.

Garton Brothers
22 Baker Road
Huddersfield HD3 3EX
Tel: 0484/33631

12 October 19..

The Chief Accountant
Tilden & Sprott Ltd
3 Grange Lane
York
YO2 5DS

Dear Sir

We have to remind you that your May account is still outstanding. You will understand that we cannot wait indefinitely for settlement.

If payment is not made within seven days we shall instruct our solicitors to recover the amount outstanding.

Yours faithfully

Mary Percy (Mrs)
Credit Controller

MP/MD/19

Exercise

Write suitable letters from the following notes:

1 *a* Pickering & Quayle, 3 March Drive, Perth, send their account
to Hamer & Co, 47 Clyde Street, Greenock. Terms—3%
discount on payment within one month.
  b Pickering & Quayle send their account for the second time.
They remind Hamer & Co of their unfulfilled promise of
payment.
  c Pickering & Quayle threaten legal action if payment or part
payment is not made within 7 days.

2 *a* Bell & Co, 327 Mount Street, Brighton BN2 1PQ, request
payment of an account of £60 from Peebles Bros, 146 Wilton
Avenue, Portsmouth PO2 8LD. Peebles Bros are valued
customers, and the delay in payment is probably due to an
oversight.
  b Peebles Bros forward cheque with a letter of apology.

3 *a* Harper & Sons, 9 Queen Street, Brighouse, Yorkshire
HD6 2RH have twice asked for settlement of the account of
Davidson & Small, 129 Thayer Road, Hull HU9 4BN. They
have to make up their books for the half-year, and wish
payment of all outstanding accounts. Write their letter to
Davidson & Small.
  b Davidson & Small apologise for delay in settling their account.
They are experiencing difficulty in obtaining payment from
customers and they promise to send a cheque in a fortnight.
  c Harper & Sons agree to wait for a fortnight, but insist strongly
on payment being made then.

4 Mr Ah Kim Boon, 284 Batu Road, Kuala Lumpur has not yet
paid his account ($550) for last month. If he wishes to be
allowed the usual $2\frac{1}{2}\%$ discount, payment must be made
within 5 days.

5 *a* Webster & Son, Beresford Street, Wembley, Middlesex
HA0 1RU have made no payment against their debt of £55
outstanding for 2 months. Until this amount has been
cleared no further orders can be accepted.
  b To the same firm 10 days later. In the absence of any reply to
the previous letter, warn them that it will be necessary to take
legal measures. As they have been customers for several years,
you would take such steps with regret.

Status inquiries

A firm which has never before dealt with a particular company may be a little doubtful of the company's good faith when they receive an opening or first order. It is customary, therefore, at the commencement of business relations, to give the name and address of at least one person or firm from whom reliable information about the company's business standing may be obtained. Alternatively, the name of their bankers may be given.

Thomas & Co
1 Greenbank Lane
Blackpool FY1 6RF

Tel: 0253-71721

JM/AC   1 May 19..

Sales Manager
Hall & Goode Ltd
21 Porter Street
Hull HU1 2RG

Dear Sir

We enclose order no 496 for electric
lamps and fittings, and would like
delivery by 15 May.

As we have not dealt with you previously,
we refer you to Messrs Smail & Son, 42
Ryse Street, Chester CH4 8HJ who will
supply you with any necessary information.

                    Yours faithfully

                    James Morton
                    (Manager)

A letter asking for information is called a **status inquiry**. Information is generally requested on the following points:

a the period of the firm's connection with the buyers
b the frequency of orders received from them
c the payment of accounts; discount allowed
d the amount of credit to be allowed

Points *a* and *b* are sometimes omitted but *c* and *d* are necessary.

Hall & Goode Ltd
21 Porter Street   Hull   HU1 2RG
Tel: 0482/69340

JD/IH/29   3 May 19..

Financial Manager
Messrs Smail & Son
42 Ryse Street
Chester CH4 8HJ

Dear Sir

We have received an opening order from
Messrs Thomas & Co of 1 Greenbank Lane,
Hull HUZ 6RF; they have referred us to you.

We should be grateful to know whether you
have had a long connection with this firm,
and whether their transactions with you
have always been settled promptly. Do
they order freely? Would you consider it
safe to allow them credit up to £400?

Any information you supply will be treated
in strict confidence. An early reply
would be appreciated.

                    Yours faithfully

                    Jennifer Duffy (Miss)
                    Credit Controller

Here is an example of a favourable reply to a status inquiry:

Messrs Smail & Son

42 Ryse Street
Chester CH4 8HJ
Tel: 0244/58712

5 May 19..

Miss J Duffy
Hall & Goode Ltd
21 Porter Street
Hull
HU1 2RG

Dear Miss Duffy

Thank you for your letter of 3 May, asking
for information about the firm whose name
we enclose.

This firm has been one of our regular
customers for the past five years, sending
us orders every three months. Payment has
always been made on the due date and all
transactions have been satisfactory.

We should be willing to allow credit up
to £400; we have in fact had several
orders from this firm for much larger
amounts.

Yours sincerely

Edward Venner
Financial Controller

EV/PH

Enc

In the reply the referee should answer carefully all the questions, but should avoid giving a definite guarantee of the integrity of the firm being discussed. It is advisable to avoid such phrases as—'You can safely give them credit up to £400'. This may constitute bad advice. It is better to say—'We should not hesitate to give them credit up to £400'. Here is an unfavourable reply about credit.

Messrs Smail & Son

42 Ryse Street
Chester CH4 8HJ
Tel: 0244/58712

5 May 19..

Miss J Duffy
Hall & Goode Ltd
21 Porter Street
Hull
HU1 2RG

Dear Miss Duffy

Thank you for your letter of 3 May, asking
for information about the firm whose name
we enclose.

Our transactions with this firm, however,
have been so small that they do not
justify an opinion from us about their
financial standing.

We are sorry that we cannot give you any
positive information that might encourage
you to do business with them.

Yours sincerely

Edward Venner
Financial Controller

EV/PH

Enc

Very often the name of the firm about which information is being given is omitted from the wording of the letter. This is done to avoid possible complications should the letter fall into the possession of any unauthorised person. In these cases such phrases as 'the firm you name' or 'the firm whose name we enclose' are used. The firm's name is typed on a separate slip of paper and enclosed with the letter.

Exercise

Prepare letters from the following information:

1 *a* Beech & Heggie, 2 Cedar Road, Wolverhampton WV3 5TY send an order for goods value £400 to White & Co, 84 Runcorn Avenue, Leicester LE3 6FD. They name Farrell & Sons, Daimler Place, Leeds LS17 0ED as a reference.
 b White & Co write to Farrell & Sons asking for the necessary information about the Wolverhampton firm.
 c Farrel & Sons reply favourably.
 d Farrel & Sons reply unfavourably.

2 *a* Mills & Co, 4 Grey Lane, Berwick ask Stevenson Bros, 69 Hull Road, York YO1 4GR for information about Trainer & Gladstone, 24 Blacket Avenue, Newcastle upon Tyne NE5 3NT who have sent them an order for £175 worth of gardening tools.
 b Stevenson Bros reply that they have had very few transactions with Trainer & Gladstone but that, to the best of their knowledge, the firm is reliable.

3 *a* A status inquiry is sent by a firm in Penang to a firm in Singapore concerning Lam Soon & Co, 42 Kim Seng Road, Singapore. Credit of $1000 is asked for.
 b The Singapore firm reply that difficulty has been experienced in obtaining payment of accounts, and they suggest that a smaller credit would be advisable.

Letters of reference

Letters of reference are another form of status inquiry where information on a specific point is sought. Opposite is an example of a letter asking for a foreign correspondent's reference. The reply is on page 102.

James Roberts & Co Ltd

14 Prince Road   Wolverhampton   WV1 1HQ
Tel: 0902/96985

CONFIDENTIAL

AJ/MM   20 January 19..

Mrs Jane Rimmer
Manager
Brown & Co Ltd
41 High Street
Sheffield S1 2GA

Dear Mrs Rimmer

Miss Jane Ayton has applied to us for a post as
Foreign Correspondent and has given us your name
as a referee. We should be grateful therefore if
you would say whether you consider her capable of
taking the sole responsibility for correspondence
somewhat varied in character, and whether her
translation of English notes into German and
French is both clear and accurate.

She speaks both languages fairly fluently, but
naturally we wish to know whether she can also
be relied upon to produce an exact translation
of the English dictated to her.

Finally, is her attitude to work satisfactory?

We should appreciate hearing from you on these
points.

Yours sincerely

Arthur Jamieson
(Secretary)

Brown & Co Ltd

41 High Street
Sheffield S1 2GA
Tel: 0742/8297

CONFIDENTIAL

JR/OF   23 January 19..

Mr Arthur Jamieson
Secretary
James Roberts & Co Ltd
14 Prince Road
Wolverhampton WV1 1HQ

Dear Mr Jamieson

We have your letter of 20 January enquir-
ing about Miss Jane Ayton.

We are pleased to say that we consider her
a first-class linguist. Miss Ayton has
been with us for almost six years, and
during the last two she has been in charge
of all French and German correspondence.
She is equally at home in both languages.

Miss Ayton is painstaking and always
thorough in her work, and may be relied
on to write business-like and exactly-
expressed letters. Her translation work
is excellent.

Miss Ayton has a pleasing and attractive
personality, and we have found her
character beyond reproach.

                    Yours sincerely

                    Jane Rimmer (Mrs)
                    Manager

Letters of introduction

A letter of introduction is a letter to introduce the representative of a firm to business houses in towns or districts to be visited. In such a letter the representative's name, his connection with the firm, and

Peel & Rose Ltd
5 Ryder Street
London EC2
Tel: 01-602-6313

Ref: JB/SM/105   15 January 19..

Messrs Frank Ezar & Sons
381 Forty-Seventh Street
New York NY 10028
USA

Dear Sirs

This will introduce Mr Ronald Blair, the
Head Buyer for the Silks and Linen Department of our firm.

Mr Blair is spending a month in the Eastern
States in order to extend our business
relations with American firms and to
cbtain new fabrics for possible introduction into our home market.

We should be very grateful if you would
introduce Mr Blair to reliable firms in
the same line of business, and if you
would give him any personal assistance
that might be necessary.

Your co-operation would be much appreciated.

Yours faithfully

John Black
Director

his reason for travelling or visiting are stated. The letter also carries a request on behalf of the representative for the advice and help of the firm addressed. There may also be mention of the firm's willingness to reciprocate should the opportunity arise. A letter of introduction is not sealed unless, of course, it is sent through the post.

Exercise

1 You have received a letter of application from Jonathan Dobson for the post of cashier/book-keeper in your firm. He has given you the name of his former employers.

   a write to them for a reference

   b as his former employer, reply favourably

2 Miss Christine Troup has been supervisor of the typing pool in your firm (a large assurance company) for six months. She is moving to another town where she has applied for a similar post. The firm in question ask you for information about her ability and character. Write:

   a a favourable reply

   b a reply, favourable in respect of ability, but pointing out a defect in Miss Troup's character

3 Write a letter of introduction to a Paris firm for your junior partner, Miss June Foster, who is to be in France for a month to establish relations with French firms.

Circular letters

The purpose of a circular letter is to give information, e.g. change of address, extension of premises, introduction of new lines, opening of a new branch, etc. It must therefore be accurate and clear.

A circular letter should be brief. If it is long, it will probably not be read; if it is short, it will in most cases at least be read. It is essential, therefore, to word the circular in such a way that the reader's attention is held from the beginning.

The following points should be included in a letter announcing the opening of a new branch:

a where, when and why the branch will be opened

b a description, attractively worded, of the stock offered

c an invitation to visit the new premises

Here is an example of such a letter:

Norse & Co

14 Main Street
Belfast BT7 1DR   Tel: 0232 688921

15 October 19..

Dear Sir

We have pleasure in informing you that,
because of the increased demand for our
sportswear in North West Ireland we are
opening a new branch of our business on
1 November at -

40 Tower Road
Omagh

We shall have on display at our new
branch a most attractive collection of
ski outfits which have just arrived from
Norway. The designs are original, the
colours bright and the prices moderate.

May we suggest an early visit to our
showroom in Tower Road? Our manager
(Mr Arthur Black) or one of his assistants
will be pleased to welcome you and show
you round.

Yours faithfully

NORSE & CO

A circular letter intimating a change in the management of a
business gives the name of the new partner, supplies a few relevant
facts about him, and states whether there is to be any alteration in

the firm's name. A continuance of the client's custom is asked for, and a copy of the new partner's signature appears on the letter. For example:

Dear Sir

We have pleasure in informing you that
we have taken into partnership Mr William
Small who has been the chief buyer in our
furniture department for the past ten
years.

Mr Small's experience and specialised
knowledge is greatly valued by the firm
and we are confident that our customers
will continue to benefit considerably.

The new name of our firm will be Sanderson, Ayre & Small and we hope that you
will continue to favour us with your
orders.

Yours faithfully

Sanderson & Ayre
now
SANDERSON, AYRE & SMALL

Mr Small will sign: W Small

When advertising goods by circular, opening on an original note may sometimes awaken the interest of the reader. Care, however, should be taken with such an opening. Study the example opposite. Note that the circular begins by asking a question in a friendly way, then come the facts, and at the end, an invitation put pleasantly. A circular written in such a way may arouse more interest than a stereotyped one, but it calls for careful presentation.

Dear Sir/Madam

STRYDEWELL SHOES

Are you thinking of a walking holiday this Easter? Of course, walking is a pleasure only in comfortable shoes; badly-made shoes can create the utmost discomfort, and may even lead to serious foot trouble.

We have produced the Strydewell shoe to meet the needs of walkers. It is made of strong but pliable box calf, and the sole is designed to give both flexibility and comfort.

We can supply this excellent shoe in various fittings, in all sizes and – most importantly – in half-sizes. It is available in black, tan, fawn, brown, and grey. The price range, we feel, is reasonable; from £24.50 to £31.50.

We should be glad to show you the Strydewell shoe at any time. Why not call in at our main shop, 69 High Street?

Yours faithfully

SMITHSONS SHOES

Exercise

1   Adebowale Stores, 8–10 Plateau Avenue, Apapa, Lagos have just had a large extension built. This extension, to be opened in two weeks' time, contains several new departments, a new restaurant, and a lounge. Write a circular from Adebowale Stores to their customers stressing the advantages of this new venture.

2   Pierce & Hogg, 8 Mornington Street, Derby DE3 4BB send a circular to customers to announce their summer sale of footwear, and enclose illustrated literature. Write their circular letter.

3   Write the following circular letters:

   a from a newly-opened greengrocer's shop to prospective customers in the district
   b from the Gas Board in your local area, giving details of a new gas cooker and offering generous trade-in terms for old cookers
   c from a sports outfitter at the approach of the cricket season to secretaries of local clubs, offering special terms of discount on purchases by clubs

Letters of application

It is essential to remember that a letter of application is normally your first introduction to a prospective employer. Your letter must therefore be clear and concise, correct and courteous. A letter badly written creates a poor impression; a neat and coherent letter with well ordered facts is certain to make a favourable impression. Therefore, keep your letter free from errors and punctuate and paragraph it sensibly. It should be handwritten unless a typewritten reply to the advertisement has been specially asked for.

Remember the importance of first impressions; plan and arrange your letter carefully. You must include certain essential facts:

   a a formal application
   b reference to the advertisement
   c your age and education
   d details of commercial/secretarial training, with a note of standards reached and examinations passed
   e any previous employment or experience
   f your willingness to attend for interview

There are, however, other points to remember about a letter of application. It is normal practice to name a referee, giving position and address where necessary. You must, of course, obtain permission before quoting a referee. Should testimonials be asked for, send typed copies *not* the originals.

It may be advisable to state the reason for leaving your present post. Do not hesitate to give the reason, but state it simply and clearly. Finally—and this is very important—take careful note of the information required by the advertisement. In your reply, overlook nothing that has been asked for.

On this and the following page are examples of letters of application. Both are for first posts, and in both, the relevant information is given in the body of the letter.

Application for the post of junior shorthand typist:

4 Radner Lane,
Newport,
S. Wales
17th April 19..

The Personnel Manager,
Messrs Hurst and Barron,
53 Wellington Street,
Cardiff
CF1 2QU

Dear Sir,

I wish to apply for the post of Junior Shorthand Typist as advertised in the 'Herald' of 16th April.

I shall be 17 years of age next month. I was educated at Poston High School and left at the end of my fourth year with three 'O' level passes in English, Arithmetic and Home Economics.

I have just completed a year's secretarial course at South Gwent College of Further Education, taking examinations in Shorthand, Typing, Elementary Accounts, Business English and Business Procedure. I have gained certificates in Shorthand at 80 w.p.m. (RSA); Typing at 40 w.p.m. (RSA); Elementary Accounts; Business English and Business Procedure.

The principal of the College, Mr W F Morton MA, has given me permission to name him as a referee.

I am available for interview at any time.

Yours faithfully,

Linda Cummings

Application for the post of secretary:

17 March Lane
Stafford
5th September, 19..

Dear Sir,

I wish to apply for the post of Secretary as advertised in yesterday's 'Evening Post'.

I am nineteen and a half years of age and was educated at St Hilda's Girls' School where I gained five 'O' level passes and one 'A' level pass in French.

On leaving school I took the Higher Secretarial Course at Middlehurst Ladies' College. This is the College's senior course and covers Shorthand, Typewriting, Accounts, Secretarial Duties, Correspondence and Communications, and Commercial French.

I have RSA passes in Shorthand (120 w.p.m.), Typewriting (Advanced), and Secretarial Duties (Stage II). In addition, I speak reasonably fluent French and have a good working knowledge of French business correspondence.

The following people have agreed to act as referees on my behalf: B Johnson Esq BA FRSA, Principal, Middlehurst Ladies College, Middlehurst, Kent and JR Martin Esq QC, The Wynd, Blackburn, near Stafford.

I am available for interview at any time.

Yours faithfully,
Doreen L James

Box No 144
Evening Post, Stafford

Remember that as you have no actual working experience it is important to emphasise your training, particularly the examinations you have passed. Later, as you gain working experience and move on from your first post, it may be preferable to give the details of your qualifications, etc., in an enclosure known as a curriculum vitae (typed by yourself) and not in the body of the letter. With this enclosure you should send a handwritten covering letter.

An example of such a letter is given below. Notice that it is in reply to a box number advertisement. An example of the curriculum vitae which should accompany it is given on page 112.

5 Queen's Gate,
Durham,
6th May, 19..

The Advertiser,
Box 115, 'Durham News',
Durham

Dear Sir,

I wish to apply for the post of Private Secretary advertised in the 'Durham News' on 4th May.

The enclosed curriculum vitae gives details of my qualifications and experience.

My present firm, Messrs Small and Peacock of 12 Bread Lane, Durham, are in the process of being taken over and, as a result, a secretarial pool is being introduced. My preference has always been to work for one or two executives. This, I feel, allows scope for one's own initiative. Therefore I am now seeking a similar type of post to that which I have held for the past four years.

You may, of course, refer to my present employer who knows why I am looking for another post.

I am available for interview by arrangement.

Yours faithfully,
Sheena Robson

Enc.

CURRICULUM VITAE

Name Sheena Mary Robson

Age 25 years (date of birth: 19.10.19 . .)

Education Calder Girls' School, Cumberland, 19 . . to 19 . .
GCE: 7 'O' levels
  2 'A' levels (English and French)
Newcastle College of Education, one year's
secretarial course, 19 . . to 19 . .
Shorthand: RSA Certificate, 140 wpm
Typewriting: RSA Certificate Stage III
(Advanced) Present speed: 70 wpm
Other certificates taken in college course:
Secretarial Practice, Correspondence and
Communications, Principles of Accounts,
Commercial French.

Experience Oct 19 . . to Aug 19 . . (2 years) Assistant
Secretary, Education Section, Carver's
Publications Ltd, Newcastle upon Tyne,
NE2 5TS. Sept 19 . . to date (4 years) Private
Secretary to Sales Director, Small & Peacock,
12 Bread Lane, Derby DE2 5LY. Present duties:
private secretarial work, conference arrangements, report and statistical work, confidential
documentation, translation work (French).

Referees Robert P Jackson QC, The Mill House,
Green Lane, Gosforth, Newcastle upon Tyne
NET 5TS.
Mr D A Illingworth, Sales Director, Messrs Small
and Peacock, 12 Bread Lane, Derby DE2 5LY.

Exercise

Write letters of application in reply to the following advertisements:

1 **Shorthand typist** required by busy advertising agency; experience in this field desirable but not essential; must be competent
in speed and accuracy; good telephone manner. Apply in writing
to Hall Advertising Ltd, 110 Wellington Place, Glasgow C2.

2 **Shorthand/audio typist** required for secretarial duties, including preparation of agenda and minutes, in central administrative office. Good salary scale, 35-hour week. Work is interesting and there are promotion prospects. Write Personnel Officer, Royal Infirmary, Leeds LS2 9LR quoting Ref RIL/SA.

3 *Wanted:* Junior for office work. Previous experience not essential. Good typing speed. Apply, with full particulars, to PO Box 68, Ikeja, Lagos.

4 *Receptionist/typist* wanted by British Typewriters Ltd. Typing, switchboard, receiving visitors and conducting showroom sales. Applicant (age about 20) must be first-class typist, have a smart appearance, cheerful personality and a pleasant voice. Salary attractive for right applicant, plus luncheon vouchers and commission on sales. There is plenty of work to do; no time for knitting. The successful applicant must be polite and efficient always, even when harassed. Write Mr J Matthews at 151 West Nile Street, Glasgow C2.

5 A progressive electronic and safety device manufacturing company requires the services of a **Confidential Secretary.** *Responsibilities:* reporting to the Director, the successful candidate must be able to perform secretarial duties with minimum supervision. *Qualifications:* applicants must be Singapore citizens who possess a secretarial diploma, have a good command of the English language and minimum of two years' relevant experience. *Remuneration:* commencing salary will be commensurate with qualifications and experience. Attractive fringe benefits.

Applicants are required to submit a comprehensive resumé together with a non-returnable photograph and contact telephone number to: The Advertiser, ST Box N81 186, Singapore.

6 **General Clerk** required. Two years' experience in general office duties. Knowledge of book-keeping preferred. Apply in own handwriting with one non-returnable photograph to: The Manager, 10A Seah Street, Singapore 7.

7 *Audio typist* wanted by incorporated insurance brokers. Applicant must have sound training/experience, with ability to write reports. Pleasant working conditions. Application in writing to: Staff Manager, Stillhouse Ltd, 10 York Place, Nottingham NG5 4PU.

8 SOUTH WESTERN HOSPITAL BOARD, SCOTLAND, Treasurer's Department—**Personal Assistant**: Applications are invited for the post of Personal Assistant to the Treasurer. Good speeds in shorthand and typing, and ability to prepare financial and statistical statements essential. The successful candidate will be responsible for the day to day running of the secretarial section of the Treasurer's Department. Post carries superannuation. Five-day week. Canteen facilities. Applications in writing with full particulars to be sent to—Secretary, South Western Hospital Board, 11 Drumsheugh Gardens, Ayr, Scotland.

Telegrams

Telegrams are normally used only in emergency. It is important, therefore, that their language should be clear and concise, but in no circumstances should clarity of understanding be sacrificed for brevity.

In a telegram all unnecessary words are omitted. The salutation and complimentary ending are dispensed with; only the essentials for understanding are stated in as brief a form as possible. Note that a telegram is typed in capitals.

Here are two examples:

1 Please meet me at 14.00 hours on Wednesday at Royal Society should be telegraphed as: MEET ME ROYAL SOCIETY 1400 WEDNESDAY MAVOR STOP

2 'I wish you to cancel our order of 8 October. A new order will be sent to you shortly'. This message might be reduced to: CANCEL ORDER EIGHT OCTOBER AWAIT FURTHER ORDER MANES AND CO STOP

Telex or telex service

This is a 24-hour teleprinter service provided by the Post Office for the speedy interchange of printed messages between subscribers in Britain and countries overseas. The Post Office rents to a subscriber (a firm, an organisation, a university, etc.) a teleprinter and a line to the nearest telex exchange. Through this exchange the subscriber can dial directly to other telex subscribers and the message from the caller is printed out simultaneously on both machines. This makes for a rapid transmission of messages.

A telex message may be sent to a subscriber even when his teleprinter is unattended. The message, as with telegrams, is in capitals and must, of course, carry the telex numbers of both subscribers. This is what a telex message looks like:

FOR: MR SUTTON
SALES
JOHNSON AND SONS
PLEASE ADD THE FOLLOWING TO OUR ORDER OF 19 FEBRUARY
6 GASKETS SIZE NO 615
5 METAL PLUGS CAT NO 421 620

HARRIS
RSES ANU CANBERRA AUSTRALIA
25 FEBRUARY 19 . .

53654 UNINEW G
RSES AA62693T

Exercises

1 The Scott Laundry Co, Hove BN3 1GF have had the contract for laundering the linen of the Lion Hotel, Hove BN3 4QY for three years. Lately the quality of the laundering has deteriorated.

   a send a suitable letter pointing this out and asking that the matter be investigated
   b reply from the Scott Laundry Co, apologising for the defects reported by the Lion Hotel. Promise to investigate the cause of the inferior work. One possible explanation is the introduction of several new staff in the package and delivery section

2 Your firm (an estate agency) is opening a small branch office. Write to a bookseller ordering a small stock of reference books.

3 You have ordered and had delivered to your home a suitcase which you are giving to someone as a present. The initials on the case have been wrongly embossed. There is, in addition, a slight dent in one corner. You are a good account customer of the shop. Write, giving details, etc.

   a your letter of complaint
   b the reply from the manager of the shop

4 Write a circular letter from the Pembroke Water Board to householders in the local area, giving notice of a temporary loss of water supply. Give the reason and specify times and details.

5 *a* Send an inquiry to Messrs Finsbury & Sons, Milton Street, Bath BA1 1LG asking why their representative has not made his usual half-yearly call on your firm (I & G Holly, Gloucester Green, Cambridge CB3 8NL). You are running short of stock and are anxious to see samples of Finsbury's products for the summer season. Specify items in which you are particularly interested.

   b Write a reply to I & G Holly, Gloucester Green, Cambridge CB3 8NL from Finsbury & Sons. Mr Hodgson, their former representative, left the firm very recently and his successor, Mr John Bray, has taken longer to make his round of their area, but is expected to be in Cambridge at the end of the month. He will have with him some new samples of items which can be dispatched at once from stock.

6 Prepare telegrams or telexes for the following messages:

   a To Cooper Ltd, Hoxton Mills, Sales, Cheshire M33 2HX, increasing the order of the previous day to 550 white towels.

   b To the Manager, Hotel Excelsior, Bukit Nanas, Kuala Lumpur 01.02 to reserve a single room with bath for three nights for Mr S K Wong, 69 Rochore Road, Singapore 7. Specify dates.

   c To a firm who have not fulfilled an order for goods by the specified date. Immediate delivery is now urgent. Supply names, etc.

7 As secretary of a large commercial organisation in London, write to the Head Office of a Trust Hotels chain asking for special terms on arrangements for your sales representatives. Stress the high frequency of their travel.

8 You have received a letter of application from Thomas Curtis for the post of finance clerk in your office. He has given you the name of his former employers; write to them for a reference.

9 Prepare a letter to Hardwell & Croft, 3–5 Green Lane, Exeter EX1 9AP asking them to quote prices for curtains for 60 bedroom windows at the New Clarendon Hotel, Dartmouth TQ7 5HW. The dimensions of the windows are 3 m by 1.1 m. Ask for recommendations of material that will be durable and washable. Patterns to be sent with quotation.

10 How to write a summary

The word précis has gone out of fashion and has been replaced by 'summary'. The dictionary defines summary as: brief account, abridgement, epitome. Précis, moreover, is defined as: summary.

A **summary** is a condensed account in narrative form of the subject-matter of a report, letter, series of letters, or any other kind of document or series of documents. It must be written in concise and clear English.

What is the purpose of a summary? Your manager, director, principal may wish to know all the important facts of a matter about which there has been considerable correspondence. He may not have the time to read all the letters and may ask you to make a summary. This summary must contain all the main points. Unimportant details must be omitted. When completed, the summary should give all essential and relevant facts of the matter under examination so that no reference need be made to the correspondence.

How brief should a summary be? This is not always easy to determine, but it should be as brief as the inclusion of all the important points will permit. Normally, one third of the number of words in the original matter is sufficient to achieve this.

All direct speech in the original matter must be turned into indirect speech in the summary. For example:

- The Chairman said, 'The situation is one of great difficulty, and we may be forced to change our attitude to shift-work.'

If the whole of this statement is to be included in the summary, it should appear as follows:

- The Chairman said that the situation was one of great difficulty and they might be forced to change their attitude to shift-work.

Characteristics of a good summary

These are as follows:

Logical order   The facts should be set out in their proper order and sequence.

Completeness   The summary must contain sufficient details to enable the subject to be understood in all its aspects without reference to the original.

Correct English   The rules of grammar must be obeyed. Slang expressions and abbreviations should not appear in a summary.

Continuity   The sentences should read easily and smoothly.

Preciseness   Care must be taken to present the exact meaning of the original.

When making a summary, try to follow these stages:

1 Read through the original, if possible twice, grasp the topic dealt with, and gain a clear idea of the subject-matter.
2 Make an outline of the summary before writing it.
3 Make a rough draft and compare it with the original; be sure you have included everything of importance and excluded all unimportant details.
4 Write the summary.

Your summary must be a summary of the whole of the original and not several small summaries of parts of the original. Therefore, do not make the mistake of writing summaries of the parts of the original and then putting them all together as one. For instance, if a particular circumstance is set out in a number of letters written over a period of time, you should not make a summary of each letter. You must grasp the main topics from all of the letters as a whole and then, in narrative form, make a summary of these topics, taking all the important details from each letter.

Economy of words is essential. Here are two examples:
● Replying to the statement of the Chairman, Mr Smith said he did not accept that view of the matter. (19)

This can be shortened to:
● Mr Smith disagreed with the Chairman's view. (7)

● It seems to me that your Company or your Directors or your Manager have shown little consideration for the special requirements of the firms for whom I am speaking. We are entitled therefore to ask that these requirements shall be more fully met in future; if not, these firms will not unnaturally seek their supplies elsewhere. (56)

This can be shortened to:
● Expressing dissatisfaction with the attitude of the Company, the speaker urged that his clients' requests receive due attention if their dealings were to be continued. (26)

Your employer may ask you to write a summary of correspondence similar to that which appears below. Could you do it? For practice, write a summary of the series of letters given below, then compare your version with the summary given on page 122.

James Russell & Co

14 Walker Street
Edinburgh EH1 2AY

17 March 19..

Miss P Wilson
Deputy Sales Manager
Messrs Henry Kay & Co
97 Park Road
Derby DE3 4HX

Dear Miss Wilson

I enclose confirmation of our order for next season's goods. Will you please give this matter your attention and deliver the order as soon as possible.

Yours sincerely

John Blythe
Purchasing Manager

Enc

Henry Kay & Co

97 Park Road
Derby DE3 4HX

```
Mr John Blythe                    19 March 19..
Purchasing Manager
Messrs James Russell & Co
14 Walker Street
Edinburgh EH1 2AY

Dear Mr Blythe

Thank you for your order for next season's
goods. It is now being dealt with and the
goods will be delivered in four weeks'time.

                    Yours sincerely



                    Penny Wilson (Miss)
                    Deputy Sales Manager
```

James Russell & Co

14 Walker Street
Edinburgh EH1 2AY

```
Miss P Wilson                    15 April 19..
Deputy Sales Manager
Messrs Henry Kay & Co
97 Park Road
Derby DE3 4HX

Dear Miss Wilson

Our customer threatens to cancel the
goods on order if they are not delivered
immediately. Can you do anything to help
us in this matter by advancing the
delivery date?

                    Yours sincerely



                    John Blythe
                    Purchasing Manager
```

Henry Kay & Co

97 Park Road
Derby DE3 4HX

Mr J Blythe   18 April 19..
Purchasing Manager
Messrs James Russell & Co
14 Walker Street
Edinburgh EH1 2AY

Dear Mr Blythe

Thank you for your letter of 15 April
expressing concern over delivery dates
for your order. We are doing our utmost
to complete your order as soon as possible and hope to send the goods by the
end of this week. I can assure you that
we have not lost any time, and I hope
the goods will be in time for your client.

                   Yours sincerely

                   Penny Wilson (Miss)
                   Deputy Sales Manager

James Russell & Co

14 Walker Street
Edinburgh EH1 2AY

Miss P Wilson   20 April 19..
Deputy Sales Manager
Messrs Henry Kay & Co
97 Park Road
Derby DE3 4HX

Dear Miss Wilson

Thank you for your letter assuring us that
the goods will be delivered by the end
of the present week. Our customer positively
refuses to wait beyond that time.

                   Yours sincerely

                   John Blythe
                   Purchasing Manager

Here is the summary that might have been written.

Summary of correspondence between Mr John Blythe Purchasing Manager, Messrs James Russell & Co, 14 Walker Street, Edinburgh EH1 2AY and Miss Penny Wilson Deputy Sales Manager, Messrs Henry Kay & Co, 97 Park Road, Derby DE3 4HX, dated 17 March to 20 April 19 . .

On 17 March 19 . . Messrs James Russell & Co, Edinburgh, placed an order for next season's goods with Messrs Henry Kay & Co, Derby, who promised to try to meet the request for early delivery. Messrs Russell & Co had not received the goods by 15 April. Mr Blythe informed Miss Wilson that their customer now insisted on immediate delivery, otherwise he would cancel the order. Mr Blythe was assured that everything was being done to arrange delivery by the end of the week at the latest.

Note that the important details from all five letters have been gathered together and summarised, so that your employer is both quickly and clearly aware of the current position.

Similarly, you may be asked to make a summary of a speech. Here is an example of a speech followed by a summary of it.

Company Chairman's Speech
This year, with a crop of 68 250 tonnes, we surpassed all previous records. This is indeed a testimony to the whole organisation at Harleston, to the field staff for having maintained high deliveries of beet to the mill, and to the factory staff for maintaining such high efficiency throughout a long crop.

At Monymusk we started the season using the old factory, which continued to operate until the completion of our large new factory. In my statement last year I anticipated that the new factory would be completed by about the end of March. In fact, it was ready on 6 April, and, having regard to all the difficulties attending such large-scale construction in these difficult times, I feel that the effort reflects great credit upon our engineers and construction personnel who achieved completion more or less in accordance with schedule. As with all new factories, experience over several crops will be needed in order to achieve the maximum standard of efficiency.

Indicative of the developments for which our company has been responsible, I would mention that 12 years ago on the areas now owned by us some 45 000 tonnes of sugar were produced in 9 old factories. In the season now commenced we hope to produce over 120 000 tonnes of sugar in 2 modern factories. I can assure you that we are keeping abreast of technical developments and that we are deriving great value from the various research units we have established.

However interesting facts and figures bearing upon the material progress made by our company may be, we must never lose sight of the fact that a proper understanding of human problems is basic to all our endeavours. We are aiming to knit together in our undertaking a team which can function in happy unity and to the maximum benefit of all concerned. This is an ideal for which we will always strive, guided by those on the spot with first-hand knowledge of the problems involved. It is not a subject which lends itself to theorising, nor indeed to modelling on patterns in other countries where different circumstances may exist. (354 words)

Summary of Company Chairman's speech
The Chairman reported that the increased output at Harleston was a testimony to the efficiency of the whole organisation. The completion of the new factory at Monymusk almost on the expected date was a tribute to the constructional staff. Full efficiency should be reached in the next few years.

Previously, the production of sugar from 9 old factories had been 45 000 tonnes; the 2 new factories should produce 120 000 tonnes. Success, however, depended upon human relationships, and the Company would continue to aim at the ideal of a spirit of unity and common purpose amongst the staff.

In this they would rely not on what happened in other countries, but on the experience and advice of those who had first-hand knowledge of all conditions in this country. (128 words)

Points to remember when writing summaries:

1 Your summary must contain all the important facts and must omit all unimportant details.
2 Its length should not be more than one third of the original.
3 Speeches and articles in direct speech must be changed to indirect speech.
4 Language and style must be simple, clear, and concise.
5 You should make your points in logical order, each leading on to the next.

Exercise

1 *Wool prices*

Once again it is advisable to appreciate that the monetary turnover is, to a large extent, governed by the price level of wool; but your directors have much pleasure in advising that during the year a substantial increase has occurred in the number of clients who are regularly purchasing part of their requirements through this company. According to all available information, wool must still be regarded as statistically very sound, but one is forced to the conclusion that there is an increasing resistance on the part of consumers to the very high prices now prevailing. This may result in an increasing use of substitutes, thus slowing up the demand for wool from the consuming centres of the world.

1 Summarise the above extract.
2 What word would you substitute for 'appreciate' in line 1?
3 What is meant by the statement that 'wool is statistically sound'?
4 Simplify the statement 'there is an increasing resistance on the part of customers to the very high prices now prevailing.'

2 Make a summary of the following correspondence:

Sadler & Co

14 Argyle Street Glasgow G2 6NT
Tel: 041 332 1968/9

```
Mr C Upton
Homes Sales Executive
Sharp & Co Ltd
35 North Street
Leeds LS6 8HT                        6 May 19..

Dear Mr Upton

Thank you for your furniture catalogue
received today. We note that you have
introduced a number of new lines, and
shall send you orders for these later.
In the meantime please forward to us:
```

3 dining-room suites No 197
4 kitchen cabinets No 35

Order no 231.

As business is brisk at present, we should
like to have these goods by 13 May.

                        Yours sincerely
                        pp Sadler & Co

                        Susan Wright

                        Marketing Assistant

Sharp & Co Ltd

35 North Street Leeds LS6 8HT
Tel: 0532/34346

Ms Susan Wright
Marketing Assistant
Messrs Sadler & Co
14 Argyle Street
Glasgow G2 6NT   8 May 19..

Dear Ms Wright

Thank you for your order of 6 May for:

3 dining-room suites No 197
4 kitchen cabinets No 35

We are forwarding these goods to you by
van tomorrow.

                        Yours sincerely

                        C Upton
                        Home Sales Executive

Sadler & Co
14 Argyle Street Glasgow G2 6NT
Tel: 041 332 1968/9

Mr C Upton
Homes Sales Executive
Sharp & Co Ltd
35 North Street
Leeds LS6 8HT   11 May 19..

Dear Mr Upton

The furniture ordered by us on 6 May was
delivered this morning. Thank you for
dealing so promptly with our order.

We regret to inform you, however, that
the glass in one of the kitchen cabinets
is cracked, and that the lock is faulty.
We shall be glad if you will send for the
cabinet and repair it, or replace it.

                    Yours sincerely
                    pp Sadler & Co

                    Susan Wright

                    Marketing Assistant

Sharp & Co Ltd

35 North Street Leeds LS6 8HT
Tel: 0532/34346

Ms Susan Wright
Marketing Assistant
Messrs Sadler & Co
14 Argyle Street
Glasgow G2 6NT   13 May 19..

Dear Ms Wright

We very much regret to note from your
letter of 11 May that one of the kitchen
cabinets delivered to you was faulty.

Our van will be in Glasgow at the end of
this week and we shall arrange to deliver
a kitchen cabinet to replace the damaged
one which our vanman will collect from
you.

We trust that you will have no cause for
further complaint, and that we shall have
the pleasure of receiving further orders
from you.

                    Yours sincerely

                    Colin Upton
                    Home Sales Executive

3 Read the following passage of about 400 words. Then, using your
own words as far as possible, write a summary of it in not more
than 140 words. Give your summary an appropriate title.

The transport of goods and passengers by air is the greatest
transport achievement of the post-war era. The great advantage
of air transport is its speed, and for this reason it is particularly
suitable for the transport of passengers. Shipping lines that once

were prosperous, with full bookings on the New York, South Africa, and Australia runs, have had to turn to cruises and the emigrant trade to earn a living. However, air transport is expensive, since aeroplanes are sophisticated technical products. Design, operation, and maintenance are all costly, and the actual pay load is small. Even the giant air-buses now coming into production carry only a few hundred passengers.

The use of aircraft as freighters has been slower to develop because the advantages of air freighting have been less obvious. Only when Air Canada began to publish its market research on air freight costs did the world wake up to the fact that air freighting was a practicable and economically advantageous method of transport for many industrial and commercial enterprises. Previously it had been thought that it was advantageous only for perishable commodities or small packets of high value, or for freight (particularly cars) directly related to passengers. Even so, the cheapest place for cargo is on the passenger aircraft.

The essential point concerning the transport of certain goods by air is that the actual cost of the air freight ticket is less than the overall cost of moving the goods from their place of manufacture to their destination. The overall cost includes many other expenses besides the actual carriage charge, two of which are mentioned below.

(a) *The cost of packing.* Packaging can be very expensive for a sea voyage, where inclement weather may damage the goods, salt air may taint produce, humidity may rust metals, etc. With air freighting most packaging is quite unnecessary. Modern aircraft fly above the clouds, nowhere near the sea, and apart from possible effects of cold, the goods in transit are unlikely to come into contact with 'weather'.

(b) *Factory condition* can be preserved. In many trades goods are finished at the factory and sent to the consumer in first class condition: dresses and suits are pressed; motorcycles are tuned; bicycles are assembled for delivery. The need to pack and ship goods destroys this sort of activity, which has to be done at the destination, with high costs of establishing depots, employing and training skilled labour, etc. With air freight, special racks installed in the aircraft enable goods to be moved in factory condition, with just a light polythene sheet over them.

London Chamber of Commerce exam. paper: Intermediate Stage

4   Summarise the following correspondence:

Angus Watson & Co

Ellison House
Newcastle upon Tyne NE1 6LH   Tel: 0632/220689

17 March 19..

Mr A P King
Paloma
Beverly Hills
California 90308
USA

Dear Mr King

Our success in selling the consignment of fruit
received from you last summer has suggested the
possibility of developing a profitable business
in tinned Californian fruit, principally pears,
plums, and peaches. We should very much appreciate your opinion of this proposition.

We presume there are fruit canneries in your
district, and, judging from the superior quality
of the fresh fruit we have had from you, it should
be quite possible to obtain a good line in tinned
fruits which would be readily saleable in England.

May we ask you, therefore, to go into the matter
for us; to give us definite particulars of the
supplies available; to send sample tins, with
prices, of each of the fruits mentioned; and to
tell us whether the quality and canning can
always be relied upon?

If the guarantee and prices are satisfactory, we
feel we can promise very considerable orders. We
shall, of course, ask you to deal with the
Californian firms on our behalf.

We look forward to having an early reply from you.
You will appreciate that we are anxious to establish this new development as soon as possible.

Yours sincerely

Sarah Murphy
Sales Director

Paloma
Beverly Hills California 90308, USA
Tel: 213/825/1768

March 31 19..

Ms Sarah Murphy
Sales Director
Messrs Angus Watson & Co
Ellison House
Newcastle upon Tyne NE1 6LH
England

Dear Ms Murphy

Thank you for your letter asking me to investigate the question of sending tinned fruits from
California to England. I assure you that I
welcome the prospect of doing further business
with you.

The fruit canning industry is already well
developed here, and I believe there is no better
product anywhere. I have sent you a sample selection from two of the leading canneries, accompanied by a fully detailed schedule of prices and
terms.

With regard to the proposed agency, I shall be
pleased to act for you on a two per cent basis,
and trust this arrangement will be acceptable to
you. I shall be able to arrange for three months'
credit and, subject to your approval, would draw
upon you at ninety days to cover the cost, freight,
and my commission.

The prices quoted for quantities will, I think,
attract you, and I am confident that the business
will prove remunerative. You may certainly rely
on the ability and determination of the canners
to maintain the excellence of the goods.

I look forward to receiving your orders.

Yours sincerely

Andy P King

Angus Watson & Co

Ellison House
Newcastle upon Tyne NE1 6LH   Tel: 0632/220689

1 May 19..

Mr A P King
Paloma
Beverly Hills
California 90308
USA

Dear Andy

The sample selection of tinned fruits mentioned in
your letter of 31 March has arrived, and it has
certainly met with our approval. It is of excellent
quality, and is certain to command a ready market
here if we can amend the prices slightly.

The selling prices, after allowing for all costs
and a small margin of profit for ourselves, are
just a little high to turn the scale in our
favour with dealers who have been stocking other
varieties; we must therefore ask you to do your
best to lower the quotation by five per cent.
If it will help you with the canners, you can
state that we expect to be able to place orders
for well over a thousand cases within the next six
months.

If you are successful, please arrange to have the
enclosed order for five hundred crates of assorted
fruits executed and shipped as early as possible,
notifying us by cable of the name of the vessel
and date of sailing, so that we can arrange the
insurance here.

To cover the value of the order, freight, and your
commission of two per cent, you may draw upon us
at ninety days and your draft will be duly hon-
oured.

Yours sincerely

Sarah Murphy
Sales Director

Cable:

MURPHY ELLISON HOUSE NEWCASTLE UPON TYNE
NE1 6LH ENGLAND FIVE HUNDRED CRATES
ASSORTED FRUITS 60 CASES S.S. AJAX SAILING FIRST
JUNE

KING

Paloma

Beverly Hills California 90308, USA
Tel: 213/825/1768

May 28 19..

Ms Sarah Murphy
Sales Director
Messrs Angus Watson & Co
Ellison House
Newcastle upon Tyne NE1 6LH
England

Dear Sarah

My cable to you dated 27 May announced the
dispatch from San Francisco on 1 June of
five hundred crates of Assorted Fruits
packed in sixty cases per SS Ajax, via
Panama.

From this you will have inferred that I
secured the reduction in price which you
stipulated, and although the canners were
very loth to reduce their earlier quotation, I was able to convince them that
the promised business was too good to
lose. I hope to hear in due course that
the shipment reaches you in time, and that
the goods meet with immediate approval
from dealers.

I have today drawn upon you, at ninety
days, for the amount of my account, as
shown in the enclosed statement.

Yours sincerely

Andy King

Enc

5 Chairman's speech at company meeting

a Summarise each of the following paragraphs giving a brief
outline of the subject matter in each.
b Write a summary of the whole speech (about 610 words),
reducing it to 200 words.

You will gather from my remarks that, compared with last
year, tea and rubber realised a higher net price. Estate costs
generally in Sri Lanka were higher and we, in common with
other owners, experienced increased production costs for both
tea and rubber. Factors which contributed to this were the
higher rate of exchange—which, of course, affected all estate
expenditure—loss of rice, increased manuring, weeding and
depreciation; also, in the case of rubber, a reduction in crop.

We do not for a moment claim that our costs are anything like
as low as we eventually hope to get them when our estates reach
what we consider their normal condition. You will remember
that when we took them over, each of the eight estates was in a
very impoverished condition, and we are having to pay the
penalty for the many years of lack of care and proper cultivation
prior to our assuming control. Only those with knowledge of
tea-growing fully realise what a long and heavy burden such
neglect entails. We are gradually overcoming the many difficulties we had to encounter, and the conditions of the respective
estates show gratifying, though in some cases slow, improvements, and augur well for continued and lasting success.

With regard to manuring, the amount spent was £8000, and is indicative of our resolve to continue high cultivation, convinced that it will result in steadily increasing yields. As old neglected fields are freed from weed growth and are cleaned and redrained, they are brought into the manuring programme, so that the item of expense is a growing one in the general working, but will give commensurate returns of crops in future years, for which we must be content to wait.

The machinery on all of our estates is kept in good running order. In addition, we are at present undertaking very large improvements to the factory, comprising the addition of two new upper storeys, which will give us the requisite accommodation for the larger crops now being obtained from this property.

We have had quantity tests taken of the water supply of this estate over a long period and find that it permits the installation of a turbine for factory power—the cheapest form of motor power there is—which will effect a material saving in the cost of manufacture. On completion of these works we hope to turn out more valuable teas.

The survey to which I referred at the last meeting has enabled us to have working plans for each estate, and has supplied us with authentic information relating to both our planted and unplanted areas. We are now able to organise properly the actual work on estates where contracts are given by the hectare, previously to a certain extent a matter of guesswork. Our estates consist of over 9600 hectares of which 2618 hectares are tea, rubber, etc., in bearing.

The remaining area includes a considerable quantity of valuable tea-growing land, some of which it is hoped, as labour permits, will be reclaimed. A start has already been made during the year. A 40 hectare new clearing has been completed, and a start has been made on a further 90 hectares. The land is all suitable, and should give good results when it reaches the bearing stage.

You will, I think, be satisfied to leave the question of what policy should be adopted with regard to the large quantity of valuable land available for tea-growing, to the discretion of the Board.

Opening new clearings is mainly dependent on the available labour, and it is unwise, therefore, to open more land unless we can secure the labour for it.

6 Write a summary of the following article (360 words), reducing it to 120 words. Give it a title.

Plans for the first really major development in the weaving section of textiles for more than half a century were revealed here today by Cassels.

The group is to spend £4 million on a new factory at Carlisle to be equipped with machinery giving 3 to 4 times the output of a conventional weaving mill. 3 other new weaving factories, all on a smaller scale, are planned by Cassels and details of these are to be announced later this year. They will all be in the north of England.

The new Carlisle plant, in which high speed 4 m wide looms are to be installed, will employ 250 people—most of them men—whom Cassels will recruit and train locally.

The choice of Carlisle for the factory, rather than one of the Lancashire cotton towns, is interesting. Carlisle has a long-standing association with textiles, but its main virtue from Cassels' point of view is that it lies within a development area, and the project will, therefore, qualify for investment grants.

The other important consideration is that in order to operate at maximum efficiency the plant will have to be run on a three-shift basis. There are therefore some advantages in taking it outside the traditional weaving areas where working practices are firmly established. Labour difficulties are unlikely, in any case, since the plans received an enthusiastic welcome from the textile union leaders.

Cassels will be anxious, during the period before the plant comes into operation early next year, to impress on their friends and customers among the established Lancashire weavers that it does not constitute a threat to them or their future.

The Carlisle plant will be used almost exclusively for weaving heavier weight cloths, covering a whole range of blends and mixtures of spun yarn, incorporating both natural and man-made fibres, for the clothing trade.

Cassels also makes the point that their new weaving plants will be closely integrated with their Northern Textiles Spinning Division, which has already announced a £12 million re-equipment programme which is said to be 'proceeding according to schedule'.

7   Write a summary of the following passage using not more than 140 words. Supply a suitable title.

The intricate pattern of commercial firms has arisen because of the need for specialisation. In a free-enterprise society people may do anything they like that is not actually criminal to earn their living. If a man sees an opportunity to offer a better service at a profit to himself he will do it, and make the profit as his reward for his efforts. This rapidly develops into a complicated network of specialist firms able to offer goods or services to the producer or consumer.

Commerce, like all other human activities, is not static, but *dynamic*. It is always on the move, always changing, always developing. It is because of its dynamic nature that commerce improves from year to year. New methods, new ideas, new materials can revolutionise commerce. What is efficient and reasonable today will be old-fashioned and expensive tomorrow compared with the new techniques that science and business research have produced.

The world commercial scene is a very complicated picture. Everyone is busy either producing, transporting or expediting the movement of goods. The producers of all this wealth are specialising in their own trades, but in return they expect to be able to purchase a selection of the goods created by other producers. The organisation required to supply us with our fair share of other people's products is complex but necessary.

Only a few people can be left out of the productive system. A few tramps, hippies and other 'drop-outs' elect to live on the fringes of life, unproductive and careless of whether they get a reasonable share of the goods produced. A few fortunate rich people do not produce, although, with taxes and death duties as high as they are, the unproductive rich get fewer year by year. The rest of us play our part in creating wealth and in consuming it. Living in a social organisation of one type or another, civilised people make laws and regulations to preserve their society.

Civilised life brings the advantages that co-operation gives to all who join in and help. If we are sick the doctor will do his best to cure us. If we need shelter a builder will erect a house. If we are cold a tailor will make a suit. If we like fast travel the engineer will make us a motor cycle, the chemical engineer will provide petrol, the rubber planter will supply the material for tyres and the glass-maker will help us to see our way with headlamps.

London Chamber of Commerce exam. paper: Intermediate Stage

8   Summarise this passage so that it could subsequently form the
     basis of a report to be written by the Company Secretary and
     circulated to branch managers of the organisation for which you
     work. Your summary should be about 170 words.

Consciously or unconsciously managers hold certain miscon-
ceptions about security as far as their businesses are concerned.
Many of them think that it is just a matter of machines and
electronics—burglar alarms, mortice locks and the like. There
are others who consider that the cost of installation of security
systems is too high and they are not effective anyway, since a
determined burglar will get in if he wants to. The third kind of
manager argues that such considerations are the function of the
specialist adviser and he should not concern himself with such
matters. What such managers overlook is that the protection of
goods, property and personnel against the depredations of
criminals is a matter which concerns everyone within the company. It is true that the 'hardware' associated with security is a
means to an end and not an end in itself, and that such
equipment is expensive. But criminals are lazy people, disin-
clined to work hard at the task and they are easily put off by the
existence of security systems. And the installation can also cause
people to be deterred from crimes other than those which involve
breaking and entering—they will feel that the company is
security conscious and so won't take risks. Most criminal activity
is not committed by thieves with oxy-acetylene cutters, but by
petty criminals, children, junior employees. For them, a security
system could merely be the provision of a light in a dim passage.
Expense has to be measured, in any case, against the fact that
changing living standards have led to a decline of morality in
society, with consequent urban terrorism and vandalism. In a
company it is a mistake to leave security to a security officer.
Each business should have a key man—a member of the board,
preferably—who actively ensures the safe-keeping of the company's buildings, stock and work in progress. The task of
checking references for new staff could also be given to him.
There are obvious ways to combat the thief, apart from the
installation of specialist equipment. There is no sense in
economising on the purchase of a safe. Barring windows is
sensible; the control of unauthorised entry is to be recommended; cash rooms should obviously not be through ways.
The use of security companies is much debated. There is a
certain public disquiet about uniformed security officers with

helmets and batons and the police have reservations about their use. But such services include overnight storage, insurance and wage packaging services as well as escort services for valuable loads and the only real alternative to their use is the provision of a sensible security system within the company itself. The administration has a responsibility towards employees as well as shareholders, and it is losing sight of both responsibilities to send young employees to the bank with cash carried in a handbag or paper sack.

Current economic difficulties heighten the use of industrial espionage and management should be aware of the extent of the danger and not simply assume that someone else in the organisation is dealing with the matter. Equipment can be installed to prevent or minimise the risk of loss of market research and data processing information; checks upon employees can prevent the loss of vital company secrets; control of entry to computer rooms, laboratories and other areas can be ensured by the issue of electronic passes. But these aids—alarms, audio systems, closed circuit television, microphones, transmitters, document shredders must not be regarded as the complete and final answer to the problem. At base, the answer lies with a trustworthy and wary professional staff. And, equally important, it is necessary that management recognise its responsibilities within the field. Security is more than a question of hardware; it is more than a matter of seeking out and receiving specialist advice; it is more than simply discounting costs involved in installation of equipment or setting them off against losses through theft. It is a matter of attitude, as well as an understanding of methods by those who have responsibility for staff and company property. And that means management—the men and women at the top.

Adapted from *Professional Administration*
Northern Counties Technical Exam. Council: English paper

Additional material for summary practice can be found in Chapter 12.

11 Minutes and reports

It is important to recognise the difference between minutes and reports. **Minutes**, in most cases, are the record of actual decisions, recommendations, and memoranda. **Reports** are written in narrative form and contain an analysis of the matter reported on, with or without recommendations.

Minutes

These are a clear, correct, and concise record of business discussed and decisions reached at a meeting. They are later approved at the next meeting of the company, club or committee when they are read by the Secretary, approved by the meeting, and signed by the Chairman as a true record. Should any alteration(s) to the minutes be necessary they should be agreed by the meeting, written in by the Secretary, and then signed by the Chairman.

In some cases the minutes may have been circulated beforehand by the Secretary and, if the approval of the meeting is obtained, they may be 'taken as read'.

For purposes of record and reference, minutes are written up in a Minute Book or in a separate File of Minutes. This record of the meeting should include:

a the date, the time, and the place of the meeting
b the names of those present (usually possible only at small meetings)
c the exact wording of any resolutions passed, and the names of the proposer and seconder

Agenda

This is a Latin word meaning things to be done. It is a list of the items of business to be dealt with at a meeting. These items are arranged in logical order so that it will not be necessary to take a later item first, which may affect a decision on one of the earlier items. Routine business is always placed first to clear the way for discussion of any special items.

Study this simple and straightforward example of a club agenda. The Secretary has called the meeting, given the place, the date, the time, and given notice of the items to be discussed. Note that any other business is often written as AOB.

Crossland Tennis Club
Dale Green
York YO2 7LS

Mr W Smith Norton   23 February 19..

Dear Mr Smith Norton

A meeting of Committee will be held in
the Clubhouse on Saturday 2 March at
5 pm.

AGENDA

1   Minutes of Committee Meeting on 10
    February 19..

2   Matters arising

3   Membership

4   Sub-committee reports

5   To authorise payment of staff pension
    to R Dobbs, Head Groundsman, in his
    retirement

6   Letter from Mr C F Meston about five
    day membership

7   AOB

                    Yours sincerely

                    R Baxter
                    Secretary

The agenda for an Annual General Meeting follows similar lines:

The Bostock Chamber of Commerce

21 Queen's Crescent   Tel: 019-225 5617
Bostock   Telex 72318

EYA/AEB   5 May 19..

<u>Education and Training Committee</u>

To all members:

The Annual General Meeting of the Education and Training Committee will be held
on Thursday 23 May at 2.30 pm at 21
Queen's Crescent, Bostock. Please let
me know on the enclosed reply card
whether you are able to attend.

                 E Y Arnold
                 (Secretary)

Enc

               AGENDA

1   Minutes

2   Matters arising

3   Correspondence

4   Chairman's Report

5   Finance

6   Election of Office Bearers

7   Joint Liaison Committee:
     a) Teacher visits
     b) Work experience for pupils
     c) Work experience for teachers

8   Next meeting

9   Any other business

Look at the minutes of the previous meeting. Remember that they must be a clear and accurate record of the business discussed and decisions reached at the meeting. They might take this form:

The Bostock Chamber of Commerce

21 Queen's Crescent　　　　　　　Tel: 019-225 5617
Bostock　　　　　　　　　　　　　Telex 72318

<u>Education and Training Committee</u>

Minutes of the Annual General Meeting
held on Thursday 23 May 19.. at 2.30 pm
at 21 Queen's Crescent, Bostock.

PRESENT:

R P Brown	Chairman
Mrs W M Dawson	Chalmers Comprehensive School
W Frame Watson	Scott College of Technology
T R Wooller	Ministry of Labour
T M White	Youth Employment Service
W Stuart Rye	Bostock College of Commerce
A E Clegg	Madson, Snead & Co Ltd
T Hunt Jones	Training Liaison Officer
Miss H Newsome	Thos Singleton Ltd
E Y Arnold	Secretary
Miss J Crowther	Secretariat

1　MINUTES

　　The minutes of the meeting held on 14
　　May 19.. had been circulated; they
　　were taken as read and signed as
　　correct.

2　MATTERS ARISING

　　There were no matters arising.

---

3   CORRESPONDENCE

Apologies for absence were received
from four Committee members.

4   CHAIRMAN'S REPORT

The Chairman reported as follows:

The Committee had met five times during
the year. Principal matters dealt with
had included liaison with the local
education authority. Both the Chairman
and the Secretary served on the Joint
Committee to establish closer contact
between schools and industry.

The Business/Teacher Liaison Scheme had
continued, and ten visits for teachers
had been arranged.

In March the Committee had assisted
with the Careers Week Exhibition
during which a panel from the Committee held advice-sessions on careers
for school leavers.

5   FINANCE

The Secretary reported on the financial
statement as at 31 December 19.. in
respect of the fund held for the payment of medals and prizes.

The accounts recorded a donation
from Mr T Hunt Jones of £10 for prizes
at the Bostock College of Commerce.

The capital sum now stood at £199.28.
The report was accepted.

6   ELECTION OF OFFICE BEARERS

The Chairman reported that he had
served his term of office and that
the Vice-Convenor, Mr W Diack, was

unable to accept the Chairmanship of
Committee because of illness.
It was agreed to invite Mr W Frame
Watson, Principal of the Scott College
of Technology, to accept the Chairman-
manship of Committee.

7   JOINT LIAISON COMMITTEE

a) The Chairman reported that ten
teacher visits had been organised
during the year. Headteachers had
written to the secretary commenting
on the success of these team visits.

b) The scheme for work experience for
pupils had been started. The first
response from firms and industry was
encouraging.

c) Difficulty was being found in
placing teachers for work experience.
An ad hoc committee was appointed to
examine the reasons for this.

Mr T M White (Youth Employment Service)
and Mr W Frame Watson (Scott College of
Technology) spoke of encouraging
results achieved by the Liaison Committee.

8   NEXT MEETING

This was left to the Chairman and the
Secretary to arrange.

9   ANY OTHER BUSINESS

There was none.

Meeting terminated 4.20 pm.

Chairman
30 May 19..

You will have noticed how the minutes of this meeting exactly followed the pattern set down in the agenda. The meeting was clearly an orderly one and accomplished what it set out to do.

Here is another example of an agenda:

```
                 BROADLANDS EDUCATIONAL TRUST

        Meeting of the Board of Governors to be
        held at 6 pm on Monday 15 September 1980.

                         AGENDA

        80/8   Minutes of meeting held 9 August

        80/9   Matters arising

               Trees adjacent to Moor Road annex
               Rewiring of Changing Rooms

        80/10  Finance Report

               (a) Operating statement: Summer
                   Term
               (b) Operating budget
               (c) Cash flow budget
               (d) Possible changes in fee
                   structure
               (e) Staff sick pay scheme

        80/11  Headmaster's Report

        80/12  Junior School: extension to
                              classrooms

        80/13  AOB

               Swimming Gala: 12 November

        80/14  Dates of next meetings

               Executive : 17 October
                           25 November
               Governors : 13 January 1981
```

In the agenda on page 145 items have been referenced showing the year 1980, followed by the item number, e.g. 80/8, 80/9 etc.

You will see from the three examples of agenda that all follow a similar pattern. It is important to remember that items for an agenda should be listed in logical sequence so that it should not be necessary—unless for some special reason—to discuss any item out of order.

Let us look now at an example of a **notice** which calls the Annual General Meeting of a company.

NOTICE IS HEREBY GIVEN that the 50th Annual General Meeting of the Abacus Transport Company Limited will be held at Abacus House, London EC1 on Wednesday 5 May 19.. at 11.30 am for the following purposes:

1 To receive and consider the Company's Accounts and the Reports of the Directors and of the Auditors for the year ended 31 December 19..

2 To declare a dividend

3 To elect Directors

4 To authorise the Board to fix the remuneration of the Auditors for 19..

5 To transact any other ordinary business

By Order of the Board
A Snow, Secretary
Abacus House, London EC1

4 April 19..

This is the form of notice generally sent by companies to their shareholders. You should again note the simplicity and conciseness of the notice.

An example of the minutes for such a meeting is given below.

Minutes of the Annual General Meeting of
members of the Don Metal Co Ltd held at
7 North Wynd, Aberdeen on Wednesday 13
June 19..
Mr A Brownlie, Chairman of the Board,
presided.

1   The Secretary read the notice convening the meeting and the Auditors'
Report.

2   The Chairman addressed the Meeting and
proposed: that the Directors' Report
and accounts for year ending 31 October 19.. produced at the Meeting, be
hereby received and adopted, and that
a dividend of 20% less income tax be
declared, to be payable to members on
30 June 19..

3   The Chairman proposed that Mr C Davidson, the Director retiring by rotation,
be re-elected as a Director of the
Company. Mr R Bronson seconded the
motion which was put to the Meeting
and carried unanimously.

4   Mr P Quentin, a shareholder, proposed
that Messrs Howell, Jones & Co, having
agreed to continue in office as Auditors for a further year, receive a
fixed fee of £... This was seconded by
Mr J Hobson, another shareholder, put
to the Meeting and carried unanimously.

5   There was no other business.

Chairman
20 June 19..

Technical terms

These are many and varied, but you will not be required to know them all. You should, however, make yourself familiar with the more common. Here are some of them:

Ad hoc   This is a Latin phrase meaning for this purpose. Therefore, an ad hoc committee is one that has been appointed for a specific purpose, to carry out a particular aim, to report back on a special responsibility. It is sometimes called a working party or special committee.

Amendment   This is a motion to alter an original motion, normally by the addition or deletion of words. Like a motion, it must be moved and seconded. If there is a vote on a motion, the amendment must be taken first.

Casting vote   This is an additional vote given to the Chairman by the rules or regulations of the company. It is used by the Chairman only when the votes for and against a motion are divided equally, so that a decision may be reached.

Co-opted member   This is a person specially appointed to act on a committee as an additional committee member, usually because he or she has some special qualification, knowledge, or experience which will be useful to the committee.

Ex-officio   This is a Latin phrase meaning by virtue of office. An ex-officio member of committee is appointed by virtue of some other position or office he may hold. For example, a trade union shop steward may, by virtue of his office, be ex-officio a member of his works Job Evaluation Committee.

Lie on the table   This is a motion proposing that no action be taken on a particular matter; in other words, that it should 'lie on the table'. It may, of course, be raised again at a subsequent meeting.

Motion   This is a formal proposal put before a meeting for the purpose of arriving at a decision. Each motion must be moved and seconded. If it is not seconded there will be no discussion on the point in question and no vote, and the motion 'falls to the ground'.

Nem con   This is abbreviated Latin for nemine contradicente meaning no one contradicting. A motion is carried nem con when there have been no votes against, although there may have been abstentions.

Next business   This is a way of ending discussion on a particular item before the meeting. The motion normally takes the form 'that the meeting proceed with the next business'.

Out of order   A statement or remark made by a member of committee is said to be out of order when it involves a breach of the rules governing the meeting.

Put the question   This is the way in which the Chairman announces the motion, e.g. 'The question before the meeting is . .'

Quorum   This is the minimum number required to be present at a meeting in order to make the meeting valid. This number is laid down in the regulations or rules of the company, association, club, etc.

Resolution   This is a formal decision arrived at by vote of the members of the meeting.

Rider   This is an addition to a resolution after it has been passed. It adds to, but does not alter the sense of the resolution, so it differs from an amendment. It must be proposed, seconded and voted upon.

Status quo   This is an abbreviation of the Latin status quo ante and means the existing circumstances.

Sub-committee   A sub-committee is appointed by the committee for a special purpose. For example, a Tennis Club committee may appoint an Entertainments sub-committee.

Unanimously   When all members at a meeting vote in favour of a motion, the motion is said to be carried unanimously, i.e. with one voice.

If you have to attend committee meetings as a member or write minutes as a Secretary to a committee it is essential that you know and understand these technical terms.

Exercise

1   Write a short paragraph on *a* minutes and *b* agenda to show your understanding of the difference between them.

2   As Secretary of your local Squash Club write a notice to your committee convening a meeting. Set out the agenda.

3   Write what could have been the minutes to the agenda on page
    146 for the 50th Annual General Meeting of the Abacus Trans-
    port Company Ltd, held on Wednesday 5 May 19 . .

4   Prepare the agenda for the Annual General Meeting of the Don
    Metal Co Ltd held on 13 June 19 . . from the minutes given
    on page 147.

5   Write the minutes to the agenda on page 145 for the Meeting
    of the Board of Governors of Broadlands Educational Trust,
    held on Monday 15 September 1980.

Reports

Reports are guides to management and organisations. The purpose
of a business report is to group together accurately, concisely and
briefly important data showing the true position of affairs relating to
a particular matter. Recommendations or suggestions may or may
not be made depending on circumstances or set terms of reference.

A report should be characterised by clear expression and neat
display. It should take the form of an argument, well reasoned and
arranged, accurate in detail, and leading logically to conclusions and
recommendations, if any.

Here are some guidelines for report writing:

1   Follow the same rules as for writing business letters, namely
    clarity, accuracy, brevity.
2   Arrange the information or argument in logical order.
3   Use indirect speech unless, of course, a personal report has been
    specifically asked for.
4   Indicate the nature of the report by giving it a heading.
5   Plan the lay-out of your report carefully, paying special attention
    to headings, paragraphs, sub-paragraphs, listed points, etc.
6   Date and sign your report.

There are two types of report:

Ordinary or **routine reports**   These are normally presented at
set intervals and pass on routine information, e.g. Chairman's
Report to the Annual General Meeting of shareholders; monthly
progress reports; financial or sales reports. They generally contain a
statement of facts. Each subject should have a separate paragraph
with relevant reference or heading.

In business today much more use is being made of forms for
routine report work.

Special reports   These are reports of a special inquiry, e.g. on

SPECIAL REPORT

                    Report of Sub-committee
                    on the siting of two
                    additional shelters in
                    the Botanical Gardens

Terms of   By a resolution passed at
reference   the Parks & Gardens Com-
                    mittee Meeting on 4 March,
                    the Sub-committee was in-
                    structed to examine the
                    siting possibilities for
                    two additional shelters in
                    the Botanical Gardens.

Action by   Three meetings were held
Sub-committee   - on 9, 17 and 25 March.
                    Two of these were held in
                    the Gardens where possible
                    sites were examined. The
                    Parks Surveyor, Mr G
                    Small, was present on both
                    occasions; his report is
                    attached.

Findings   1. Several good sites are
                    available, two in the
                    South Garden and one in
                    the Palm Grove, as shown
                    on the enclosed plan at
                    A, B, and C.
                    2. All three are suitable,
                    but siting at B would
                    result in the loss of
                    some very valuable shrubs.

Recommendations   That one shelter be sited
                    in the South Garden at A,
                    the other at C in the
                    Palm Grove.

                    Signed

                                James Clarke
Encs   Convener

accidents, fire damage, staffing, etc. They may also be reports from a sub-committee appointed for the specific purpose of examining an item or requirement and reporting back to a main committee or authority (see page 151).

The content of any special report is determined by its **terms of reference,** i.e. the instruction or guide governing the report. In many cases such terms of reference come direct from the Minute Book.

When writing a special report the terms of reference should be stated first; facts and arguments should then follow in logical order—all such facts and arguments must be relevant to the terms of reference—then come the findings; and finally the conclusions and recommendations. The report must also be signed and dated.

Let us look now at a more complicated and detailed special report from a sub-committee appointed to investigate and report on the decline of trade in the Birmingham area.

REPORT OF SUB-COMMITTEE

Appointed in terms of a resolution of the
Board passed on 5 Feburary 19.. to
investigate and report on the decline of
trade in the Birmingham area.

Resolution That a sub-committee be
appointed to investigate and report on the
decline of trade in the Birmingham area
for the period ending 31 December 19..
and to make recommendations.
That the sub-committee consist of the
Chairman (Mr Fergus Anderson), Mr Robert
Burton and Mrs Jenny Blackwood.

Report by Branch Manager A summary of
the written report furnished by the
Branch Manager gives the following particulars: 1. During the past twelve months,
ten of our large customers have volun-
tarily ceased business operations, whilst
three have been compelled to go into
liquidation, owing to inability to meet
their commitments. Our former trade with
these people represented in round figures

£15 000 per annum. 2. Competition has
increased considerably, especially in the
goods supplied by Department G. 3. Trade
has been unstable and otherwise unsatis-
factory during the year, largely due to
general trade depression and unofficial
strikes. 4. Other firms in the London
goods trade have had to record similar
losses, e.g. Harold Lloyds & Co, William
Garrick & Murray, Campbell, King & Co.

<u>Chairman's visit to Birmingham</u> On receipt
of above report Mr Fergus Anderson visited
Birmingham on 14 February and inspected
the branch. He observed the operations of
the staff, inspected the books, called
upon several customers along with the
representative and discussed with the
latter the points referred to in his
report.

<u>Branch Manager at Head Office</u> At our
request the Branch Manager came to London
on 21 February, and the sub-committee
discussed the situation with him.

<u>Other investigations</u> The sub-committee
has made investigations in other direc-
tions, notably in the chief departments
doing business in the Birmingham section.
It has also addressed inquiries to com-
petitors and trade agencies; perused
representatives' reports; and consulted
information from other sources. Five
meetings have been held, and the sub-
committee now submits the following
findings.

<u>Findings</u>

1 The report of the Branch Manager is,
   in the main, correct.
2 The staff in the Birmingham branch are
   inadequate.

3 The Branch Manager personally attends
   to too much detail and subsidiary work
   and, as a result, the branch requires
   reorganisation.
4 The premises are inconveniently situa-
   ted and somewhat unsuitable for the
   present style of business.
5 There is a need for more discrimina-
   tion in Department A in respect of
   certain classes of goods.

Recommendations

1 New premises should be found at the
   earliest opportunity.
2 The duties of the Branch Manager should
   principally be obtaining orders and
   supervising the branch.
3 Staff and their duties must be re-
   organised.
4 Monthly comparison of sales reports
   should be sent to the Branch Manager.
5 The Branch Manager should forward his
   reports monthly and not, as at present,
   quarterly.
6 Some investigation should be made into
   the qualities and designs offered by
   Department A.
7 The question of this branch should be
   reconsidered six months from this date.

Data Detailed data relevant to this
Report is attached.

31 March 19..

Signed: Fergus Anderson, Chairman
        Robert Burton
        Jenny Blackwood
        James Thomson (secretary)

When writing reports always be logical, relevant, and unbiased.

Memorandum

A **memorandum** or **memo** is a short and informal note, report or message, generally written on a specially printed form for circulation within a company. It is used for brief messages, e.g. dispatch of goods, receipt of formal communications, appointments, etc. Printed forms vary but they follow this pattern:

Memorandum

From: Sales Manager   To: Advertising Manager
Ref: SM/141/A   17/11/19..

Attached report for your comments, by
30/11 please.

SM

Enc

Exercise

1   What is a business report? How does it differ from minutes?

2   Your employer wishes to close the firm's canteen. He states that it is not being sufficiently patronised and that he would prefer to issue luncheon vouchers. He asks you to write a report on this.

3   As assistant to the Personnel Manager you have been asked to write a memo complaining about the poor standard of cleaning in the office. Address your memo to the Cleaning Supervisor.

4   Your employer is considering introducing flexitime in your office. Write him a report setting out the advantages and disadvantages.

5   Find out as much as you can about word processors and write a short report for your Office Administration Manager describing why your firm should (or should not) install one.

12 Comprehension

Comprehension and interpretation of a passage means understanding and explaining what has been written. Interpretation goes much further than paraphrasing; nevertheless, successful interpretation depends largely upon the ability to paraphrase, but you need to understand something before you can paraphrase it.

The dictionary definition of **paraphrase** is: to express in other words. Here are some guidelines to help you when paraphrasing:

1 Read the passage carefully and slowly more than once; if possible read it aloud.

2 At your second or third reading paraphrase in your mind each sentence.

3 Read the questions set, paying attention to the *exact* requirements of each.

4 Find the section of the passage that answers each question. The material used in your answer must be found in the subject-matter, except when a personal opinion is asked for.

5 Answer in properly constructed sentences and, unless instructed otherwise, in your own words. Single words or short phrases from the original, if simple and in common use, may be used, but not the repetition of whole sentences.

6 When asked to give the meaning of words and phrases as used in the passage, make sure that those you set down can be substituted for the original. In this type of answer sentence form is not necessary.

7 If asked to suggest a title to the passage, leave this answer until you have attempted the other questions; in this way you will find it easier to provide a suitable title.

8 Refer to a dictionary for the meaning of any unfamiliar words.

Here is a passage followed by some comprehension questions. The answers are given after the questions. Try to answer the questions on your own without referring to the answers. Then use the answers as a check against your own.

Learning at a distance

The Open University provides higher education for home-based students using a *multi-media approach to learning*. The central elements are the correspondence texts, written by full-time staff, and the assignments which are despatched to students regularly throughout their courses. The correspondence texts and assignments are associated with radio and television broadcasts transmitted throughout the teaching year, and *optional tutorial and counselling sessions* are arranged with members of the University's part-time staff in local study centres. In addition some courses (including all the foundation courses) have an obligatory one week *residential* summer school which provides an opportunity for more intensive study under personal supervision.

Each of the foundation courses lasts from February to November and involves an average of twelve to fourteen hours' work each week.

There are two ways in which the part-time staff are involved in tuition: firstly, they criticise and assess by correspondence the *written assignments* sent in regularly by students; secondly, they take part in the optional tutorials with students at a local study centre. The University aims to be more than a correspondence institution whose students are *learning in isolation*. One of the advantages of a conventional university is the opportunity for academic discussion between students and staff. By supplementing the direct teaching method of correspondence material with the more personal tutorial and study groups based on local centres, the Open University attempts to offer additional support for those students who are in a position to take advantage of such *interaction*. The summer school enables students to broaden their ideas by contact with staff and other students and to gain valuable experience in, for example, laboratory work.

Assessment of what has been learnt during the course is undertaken in two ways: throughout the year assignments submitted by students are commented upon, assessed and returned, and a three hour examination is taken at the end of the course. Two forms of assignment are used: written questions and essays assessed by the tutors (tutor-marked assignments called TMAs), and objective tests which can be marked by computer (computer-marked assignments known as CMAs). A credit is awarded on the successful completion of the course, based on the combined results gained in the end of year examination, and the best marks obtained in both forms of assignment.

Open University Handbook

1 What do you understand by the words 'multi-media approach to learning'?

2 Explain the involvement of part-time staff in Open University tuition.

3 Explain briefly the purpose of the obligatory summer school.

4 What are the two forms of assessment used?

5 Explain in their context the meaning of the following words and phrases:

   a optional tutorial and counselling sessions
   b residential
   c written assignments
   d learning in isolation
   e interaction

6 Suggest another title for this excerpt.

Your answers might follow this pattern:

1 This phrase means that the Open University provides several approaches to learning through different methods; namely, by correspondence units, through radio and television programmes, by face-to-face tutorial and counselling meetings, and by written work submitted for assessment.

2 Part-time staff hold tutorial groups and counselling sessions at study centres; they also assess and comment on the written work submitted by students.

3 The summer school gives students the chance of face-to-face discussion with staff and with students from other areas, thereby providing the opportunity for detailed and concentrated study. Also, in certain courses, practice in laboratory and project work is provided.

4 The two forms of assessment are:

   a TMAs i.e. tutor-marked assignments which are written tests marked and assessed by tutors.
   b CMAs i.e. computer-marked assignments which are objective tests checked by computer.

5   *a* learning sessions, attendance at which is not obligatory
    b living-in
    c written work—questions, essays, projects, etc.—sent in for assessment
    d studying completely on one's own
    e exchange of views and ideas

6   An experiment in learning.

Now try to answer the questions on the following passages in the same way.

All weather sports pitches

A British firm has developed an artificial sports surface, suitable for most games, which it is hoping to introduce into Africa where climatic conditions make it difficult to maintain a natural pitch. The surface, Tufturf, has been developed as a result of six years of *combined expertise* from ICI, British Ropes, and Crossley Carpets.

Mr John Lancaster, Managing Director for the marketing company Tufturf, said that the new surface was particularly suitable for hot countries where sports are normally played on hard and therefore dangerous grounds. Basically, Tufturf gives a much better *playing surface*. As a result the bounce of the ball is much more predictable and this clearly puts the emphasis on skill. It provides the finest *artificial wicket* and, as a football ground, it would obviously not be subject to bad weather conditions.

Tufturf is cheaper than those of rival companies and *carries a guarantee*. It has been approved by FIFA (the world football governing body) and by Britain's Sports Council. Several British football clubs are already using this surface, and a practice net surface of Tufturf has been installed at Trent Bridge, Nottingham's county and test match cricket grounds.

The surface can also be laid on patios, poolsides, roof gardens, and on putting greens. It can be cleaned either *by hosing down* or by vacuum cleaner. It can be used for any sport in which spiked shoes are not needed, and because of the uniformity of bounce that it provides, can be bettered only by a perfect natural playing surface.

Tufturf is made by ICI's top grade ultraviolet *stabilised* polypropylene. This means that there is no danger of *friction burns*; also, the substance does not absorb dirt from moisture.

Adapted from World Peace Magazine, Nigeria

1 Comment briefly on the choice of name for the product Tufturf.

2 How would you explain 'combined expertise'?

3 List four main qualities of Tufturf.

4 What, in your view, would constitute 'bad weather conditions' in Africa?

5 Why is the bounce of the ball on Tufturf important?

6 Explain the following words and phrases:

   a playing surface
   b artificial wicket
   c carries a guarantee
   d by hosing down
   e stabilised
   f friction burns

7 Suggest another title for this passage.

Shop talk

A modern department store can offer you a wide choice of careers.

You can progress quickly if you have that special combination of liveliness, enthusiasm and drive which often proves more important in your career than academic attainments alone. If, in addition, you have academic attainments, then today's *retailing* offers you as rewarding a means of using your abilities as you will find anywhere. Unfortunately many young people tend to shy away from the retail trade because they feel there is nothing more to it than standing behind a counter and wrapping up parcels for customers. But if you have *a gift for selling* or have been carefully trained, then you will take pleasure in making every customer feel that he or she has enjoyed buying something from you.

If you like choosing and wearing exciting clothes, you may feel that you could *show the average fashion buyer a thing or two* that would transform the whole department into something spectacular. But you need to spend several years on the selling floors learning to understand every aspect of *modern merchandising* before you would be ready to take on the enormous responsibility of investing many thousands of pounds of the store's money in goods which must sell quickly if you are to have enough money to *re-invest* in next season's stock.

In an increasing number of group-stores you will also have learned to interpret the long columns of computer data which, properly used, can give a buyer a clear picture of the success or otherwise of the various items in the range.

But these are just two of the career areas that are open to you. In fact you could say that there is more of everything in retailing. First, there are more people because it is one of the largest employers in the country. Second, there is a great variety of jobs, ranging from selling to systems analysis, from buying to *budgetary control*, from staff management to *stock control*, from display work to data processing, from catering to credit management. Third, its *management to staff ratio* is one of the highest in any occupational field, which means that promotion prospects are very good.

Above all there are the glamorous, even dramatic, aspects of working in department store surroundings which are designed to show off a bewildering array of merchandise from all over the world.

Adapted from *School Leaver*

1   List a few of the careers offered in a modern department store.

2   What is meant by 'retailing'?

3   The writer makes the retail trade sound an exciting prospect for jobs for young people. Explain how he does this.

4   What is meant by 'management to staff ratio'?

5   Explain the meaning of these words and phrases in context:

   a   a gift for selling
   b   show the average fashion buyer a thing or two
   c   modern merchandising
   d   re-invest
   e   budgetary control
   f   stock control

6   Suggest another title for this passage.

Another feather in SSE's cap

Singapore Shipbuilding and Engineering Limited has added another feather to its cap with the completion and delivery of the 7500 *tonne container ship*, Pegasia, for West German shipowners, Wilhelm Harms and Jonny Gahrs of Hamburg.

The ship is part of a contract worth more than $120 million to build 10 ships—the biggest single contract ever won by a local shipyard. The Pegasia is the first of the ships to be delivered to the owners. It is the first vessel to be built locally to meet the *exacting requirements* of the West German Government.

SSE won the *multi-million dollar contract* after stiff competition from Japanese, South Korean, and European shipyards.

The managing director of SSE, Mr Thomas Ng, said: 'We are proud to build this ship as it is one of the most sophisticated vessels to be built in Singapore. It is the latest generation of container ship designed by a West German firm of consultants'.

He said the actual construction time for the vessel was about a year. The ship is designed as a container ship but can be easily adapted for general cargo. *'If the container market is bad*, the vessel can be used for carrying other types of cargo. Its *capacity utilisation* is more than in an ordinary ship', he said.

The Pegasia measures 120 metres long and is able to carry 400 containers. It has a *service speed* of 15 knots. It operates on a full-automation system and is fitted with a fail-safe device.

Most of the equipment that went into the construction of the Pegasia came from Japan except for the propeller system which is from Sweden. The machinery pieces were brought from Nissho-Iwai of Japan on a *package basis,* thus saving the shipyard a lot of research time.

This is the first time that a local yard has bought equipment on a package basis, according to Mr Ng. The propeller system is from Kamewa of Sweden and together with the bow thrust unit fitted in the ship's forward, the vessel is extremely manoeuvrable. Besides the other nine container ships, SSE has orders at hand to keep its workers occupied for several years.

The Straits Times, Singapore.

1   Explain the word 'tonne'.

2   'The Pegasia is one of the most sophisticated vessels to be built in Singapore.' What does the Managing Director mean by this?

3   What is meant by a 'container ship'?

4   In one short paragraph describe the Pegasia.

5   Explain the meaning of the following words and phrases as they are used in the passage:

a exacting requirements
b the multi-million dollar contract
c if the container market is bad
d capacity utilisation
e service speed
f a package basis

6 Suggest another title for this passage.

Business as usual

'I wonder if you could come down next weekend?'

'I'm *in conference* all Tuesday.'

'Wednesday, then?'

'I'd be delighted. Could you pick me up at the club?'

'Athenaeum?'

'My dear fellow, no, that Heathrow place. I'll be flying in: conference in Geneva.'

'What flight?'

'My own—I've just got a most interesting new swing-wing.'

'VTOL?'

'Hardly—a new method we'll be marketing quite soon.'

'I'll send a Rolls.'

'How can we contact you?'

'My cars are fully equipped. You just call PRO/PD on your radio—the *wavelength* is in the international confidential file: I presume you have it?'

'My organisation prints it.'

'Fine, Wednesday then; bring your golf clubs.'

'I'll get a set when I turn up.'

'But, my dear chap, can you manage without your own?'

'They'll be my own—VK47 Jackobusters. He designed them for me, *now they're on the market*.'

The Sussex cottage stood in its owner's grounds, which were not small since he had bought up three surrounding farms to ensure a proper seclusion. The *private heliport* on what had been the village cricket field was for some reason still resented. As the Rolls crossed the invisible beam the wrought-iron gates slid noiselessly open while the plastic coats of arms which adorned them were discreetly illuminated from inside. The Georgian front dated back to at least 1928 and behind it in parts of the house there still were traces of its sixteenth century origins. As Sir Herbert was assisted from the Rolls, the front door was opened. Bunbelly, the travelling butler, who always did for Sir William at weekends, *bowed comfortably*. Sir Herbert was offered a wash. (There was only a rather small and *indifferent Picasso in the loo*, he noticed.)

Spectator

1   At which elements of the business world does the writer poke fun?

2   How does the writer poke fun at the top-level business executives? Try to describe his method.

3   What is the effect of the dialogue? Do you think it is successful or not? Give your reasons.

4   Choose two short extracts from the passage and say why you think they are funny.

5   Do you think that the writer is being fair in his picture of businessmen at work?

6   What do you understand by the following words and phrases?

   a in conference
   b wavelength
   c now they're on the market
   d private heliport
   e bowed comfortably
   f indifferent Picasso in the loo

7   Suggest another title for this passage.

The tycoon's world

If you are a *breathless young businessman* on the make, half-way to your first million pounds, you need a telephone in your car, *Girl Fridays* about the place and a business jet at London airport. The idea is that tycoons must spend as much of their time on tycoonery as possible. They must not waste it in airport lounges. *Secretaries or electronic equivalents* must always be available—no question of hanging about waiting for your girl to come back from lunch-time shopping in Oxford Street. Thus a whole new industry has sprung up which specialises in services, *gadgets and gimmickry for whiz-kids*.

Here are some of the facilities currently available. Arriving at Heathrow on a scheduled flight, first class, *our young tycoon* changes into his own jet. If you hire it from Executive Jet Aviation the cost is £3 per mile, £500 minimum charge per flight. The Lear jet has seats for six passengers, plus pilot and co-pilot. Unfortunately no hostesses are provided—you have to bring your own. The sales argument is that private jet travel is essential for 'men to whom a matter of minutes can make the difference between failure and success'. Well, I wonder about that. Do many business deals depend upon split-second timing? I must also issue a warning. None of the business jets in which I have travelled are at all comfortable. It is speed and convenience you are buying rather than luxury.

There are about 2000 business jets in use throughout the world. Of these, more than half are in the United States, the remainder scattered throughout the world. To buy a business jet can cost up to £600 000 plus the high cost of airport charges, maintenance facilities and the employment of two internationally qualified pilots. It is, therefore, sometimes more economic to hire a jet than purchase one. Executive Jet Aviation's 700 mph Lear jets are spread throughout Europe and can be summoned at any time by Telex, or through a telephone call with the aid of a special identity card. EJA is even willing to put the customer's name on the side of the plane.

Spectator

1 Do you think the writer is serious or not? Give reasons for your answer.

2 How would you describe the writer's attitude to 'tycoonery'?

3 Give your definition of 'tycoonery'.

4 What do you think the writer means by the following words and phrases:

  a breathless young businessman
  b Girl Fridays
  c secretaries or electronic equivalents
  d gadgets and gimmickry for whiz-kids
  e our young tycoon

5 What is the writer's opinion of private jet travel? What are the reasons for this view?

6 Give this excerpt another title.

Prospects bleak for business graduates

The job market is suffering from *a glut of business administration graduates* because the number of jobs has failed to increase proportionately with the graduate output from the University of Singapore.

A business administration lecturer in the University of Singapore, Mr Tan Thiam Soon, gave this warning in an article in the *Singapore Manager*, published by the Singapore Institute of Management. He said business graduates have to fight with others, perhaps from economics or engineering courses, besides competing with their counterparts.

Multinational corporations and large local companies, the main employers of business graduates, are limited in number and would not be able to absorb many graduates.

Job opportunities in the *public sector,* moreover, are diminishing as the government has recently announced that the majority of new jobs to be created in the next five years would be in the *private sector.* The alternatives are employment in small firms or in their own business ventures, for both of which, however, the university product is not geared because of *the nature of its courses*.

Mr Tan suggested a partnership between the university and business community to give the business undergraduate both theoretical and practical knowledge and to inculcate in them '*the right perspective* of working for a small firm and the opportunities and challenges associated with it'.

Commercial concerns, especially small firms, should allow business undergraduates to be attached to them for short periods, during which they would learn and understand the practical problems of running a small business. 'In order not to upset the operation of the firms, the attachment programme can be arranged on a part-time basis during the first six months of the final year of study in the university', Mr Tan wrote.

At the same time, the student can act as 'apprentice consultant' to the firm under his lecturer's guidance by suggesting to owner/manager how to improve the firm. 'In this way, the gap between theory and practice can be bridged, and the student will be able to put into practice and test the validity of the knowledge acquired in the classroom', Mr Tan explained.

Through such a *theoretical-cum-practical course* the graduate will be better equipped for jobs and perhaps more receptive of lesser-paid jobs in small firms with growth potential.

Even if, upon graduation, the student joins a large company, the practical experience thus acquired would make him more mature in his dealings. Besides, small firms offering such attachments would also benefit from the management consultancy of the graduate. They may not be able to afford *expensive expertise*.

Mr Tan also suggested that money-lending institutions could ensure that small businessmen, to whom they lend, are properly assisted by arranging with the universities for business graduates to be attached to such companies.

The Straits Times, Singapore

1 In one short paragraph, in your own words, explain the warning given by Mr Tan Thiam Soon.

2 What do you understand by 'multinational corporations'?

3 Explain what is meant by 'the public sector' and 'the private sector'.

4 What is the purpose behind Mr Tan's suggestion for a partnership between the university and the business community?

5 Mr Tan proposes a way whereby the gap between theory and practice can be bridged. Explain briefly this proposal.

6 What do you understand by the following words and phrases?

   a a glut of business administration graduates
   b the nature of its courses
   c the right perspective
   d theoretical-cum-practical course
   e expensive expertise

7 Suggest a different title for this passage.

Partnership in the office

All men and women in responsible posts face business life together with their secretaries. How effective the partnership is depends *on many factors*, but there can be no doubt that any time, thought and energy used in making the partnership work is well rewarded.

The first priority of an executive is to organise the services necessary to him so that his time and *creative thinking* can achieve the best results possible: in other words, to create productive time.

There is an old saying that 'A first-class secretary can make an average executive look good; but an average secretary can make a first-class executive look very mediocre'.

Executives of all levels today are working in an atmosphere of ever-increasing pressure. Many of them already have secretaries who, given the opportunity, are anxious to play their full part and do all they can to help their chief carry out his or her real function, which is often essentially creative. It is *paradoxical* that so many able men and women executives are hampered in their work because of the lack of good secretarial help, while at the same time there are many able, keen and conscientious clerical workers and secretaries who drift from job to job seeking work that will give them some satisfaction.

In my experience secretaries seldom complain of overwork, but all too frequently they do complain of *a sense of frustration*, because for a variety of reasons their chiefs make it difficult for them to do a job which is satisfying and worthwhile to themselves or to anyone else.

One of the biggest mistakes made by executives when choosing a secretary is revealed by a glance at *daily vacancy columns in the press:* if one did not know anything about business life, it could easily be assumed that every executive needed the same kind of secretary and that the duties of every secretary were alike—nothing is further from the truth.

If the partnership is to work to the advantage of both members of the team, it is necessary that the secretary and her chief should understand *each other's role.* Each secretarial job is different, for each depends on the personalities of the people involved, as well as the kind of work they do.

You and Your Secretary The Industrial Society

1 In your own words explain what you consider to be the first priority of an executive.

2 Explain, in one short paragraph, what is meant by the 'old saying' quoted in the third paragraph.

3 What does the writer mean by 'paradoxical'?

4 'Each secretarial job is different.' Do you agree? If so, give your reasons.

5 What do you understand by the following words and phrases?

    a on many factors
    b creative thinking
    c a sense of frustration
    d daily vacancy columns in the press
    e each other's role

6 Give the passage another title.

Training for today's jobs

'It is all right to set your sights high. Work hard, gain a good education, reach for the stars. But settle for what you can be. Not everybody is going to be an *astronaut*. And what's more, settle for the jobs that are going and not the jobs you think ought to be there.' Who said that? It was Lee Kwan Yew, Premier of Singapore. Lee Kwan Yew's theme is that there is a *tendency today for people to aim beyond their potential*. We could also say that, in general, it is still true that craft, industry, manufacture are given far too little prominence in the educational scheme, although manufacture, export, specialised craft services are the *lifeblood of the economy*. We could add that reverence for the *purely academic and theoretical* still remains a powerful force in education.

We do not mean that this should not be so. We take the view that the *ascertainable* needs of our economy this year, next year, and as far ahead as we dare estimate, should be an equally powerful force in educational thinking. Suppose we now relate these ideas to what is happening in our own education, the training of young people to play a valuable and a progressively more rewarding part in the business of the country, especially in the offices.

Some young people undoubtedly leave us with their full potential unrealised. Some others leave us having tried to reach a level of attainment that is beyond them. Their intelligence and their ability to learn more is beyond their capabilities. Whether we are training people for the jobs that are there is not a problem to us. We know they are there. In the larger urban areas, the demand continuously exceeds the supply.

Are we training young people for the jobs that will be there next year and in a few years' time? We are training people to become office communications operatives. Is there the chance that within a decade or two, 'word-processing' will change or even eliminate the need for the sort of *curricula* that we work on now? It would be a bold person who answered a flat 'No'. Who would have said at the end of the Second World War that men would walk on the surface of the moon within 25 years?

What we surely have to do is to keep our eyes and ears open to every technological advance that may affect our field, and to gain all the personal modern office experience that we can. At the moment we are, with some reservation, on the right lines. The closer we can make *the rapprochement between industry and commerce and the educational world* in our own areas a reality, the greater the chance we have for training people for the jobs that are there, and the jobs that will be there in four or five years' time. Beyond that we really need a *crystal ball* that works!

Office Skills, Pitman

1   In your own words say what you understand to be Mr Lee Kwan Yew's advice.

2   Explain in more detail the following:

   a 'tendency today for people to aim beyond their potential'
   b 'purely academic and theoretical'

3   What views does the writer hold about the training for jobs for young people now and in the years ahead?

4   What does the writer mean by 'the rapprochement between industry and commerce and the educational world'?

5   Explain the following words and phrases as they are used in the passage:

   a astronaut
   b lifeblood of the economy
   c ascertainable
   d curricula
   e crystal ball

6   Find another title for this passage.

Practice papers

1 Correct, where necessary, these sentences; explain the reasons for your corrections.

   a Whom do you believe him to be?
   b He is more business-like than me.
   c Neither the manufacturer nor the wholesaler were to blame.
   d You must forbid him coming.
   e I should be glad if you will reply at once.

2 Write sentences, one for each word, to show that you understand the difference in meaning between the words in each pair:

   uninterested; disinterested   annoy; aggravate
   perpetrate; perpetuate   practical; practicable
   luxurious; luxuriant   affect; effect

3 Write a well-constructed paragraph of approximately 100 words on the main elements of a good business letter. Then write a sample business letter ordering various items from a firm in Ireland.

4 You have received an opening order to the value of £200 and have been given the name of a firm as reference.

   a Write the status inquiry to the firm (supply names and addresses).
   b Write the status reply (favourable).

5 A firm of manufacturers in Scotland is sending one of its directors to attend the Canadian Trade Fair in Toronto in order to promote sales. Write a letter of introduction to a firm in Toronto on behalf of the director (supply names and addresses).

6 You have sent to a mail order firm for a cassette-recorder, with two spare cassettes. When the parcel arrives you find that the package is badly torn and that only one spare cassette has been sent. Write a letter to the firm giving details of the damage and pointing out that one spare cassette is missing. Ask the firm to let you know what you must do to have the matter put right.

Paper two

1   Use the following words in sentences to distinguish their meaning clearly:

deprecate, depreciate; differ, defer; precise, concise

2   Blane & Co, Lancaster (telegraphic address BLANECO, Lancaster) send a telegram to McConnell & Co, Belfast (telegraphic address LINEN, Belfast) asking them to increase their order no 363 to 245 men's handkerchiefs. Delivery is urgent. Write out the telegram of 12 words or less. Also, write the reply.

3   Parke, James & Co, Harper Street, Newcastle upon Tyne NE3 5QH send the following order to Midland Tools Ltd, Coventry CV3 8EB:

1 Lathe—surfacing, sliding and screw-cutting as shown on p 10 of catalogue no 6

to be sent by goods train, carriage forward to their address. Delivery within one month. Write the order letter; also the letter acknowledging the order.

4   Study the following examples of business jargon and re-write each one in simple and direct language:

a your esteemed favour to hand
b we beg to acknowledge receipt of your communication
c we thank you for same
d we beg to assure you
e we enclose herewith
f it is felt to be necessary
g we shall take a very early opportunity of writing
h it has been brought to our notice

5   Add the correct prepositions to the following:

agree; deficient; inspired; intrude; ineligible; correspond; prevail; responsible; wait; call; part; disappointed

6   Write a reply to the letter shown opposite. Here are some notes to help you write the reply:

a goods were dispatched by carrier immediately and should have arrived by now. There was a hold-up at carrier's depot
b materials charged on returned bill were sent. A receipt signed by warehouseman is held by Technical Supplies Ltd

Hallwin & Edgar

421 Oxford Street London W1R 1RF

Mr G Cummins
Home Sales Manager
Technical Supplies Ltd
Bermondsey   13 May 19..

Dear Mr Cummins

We were very surprised when, after our talk
with you yesterday, the goods which you had
promised would be sent off immediately did
not arrive this morning. This is by no
means the first time that we have had to
complain about delay on your part in ful-
filling orders. Less than six months ago
we made a similar complaint. Although we
know that the materials you supply are as
good as you claim, punctual delivery is as
important to us as quality, since we
cannot retain our customers unless we can
fulfil all their orders without delay.

There is one other matter to which we
should like to draw your attention. Three
days ago we received the enclosed bill, in
which we are charged for materials that
have not been supplied. We shall be glad
to have your explanation.

We hope that both these matters will
receive prompt attention and that we shall
not have to take our business to any other
firm for, as you know, we have a high
opinion of your materials.

Yours sincerely

Michael Green
Purchasing Manager

Enc

Paper three

1 *a* Give a synonym for each of the following words:

despatch; assent; achieve; construct; plan; apparent; concise; prevalent

b Give an antonym for each of the following words:

sever; calm; assemble; general; illicit; careful

2 Using your knowledge of expression and style comment on each of the following pairs:

a a pocket watch; a watch pocket
b man is vile; the man is vile
c he only borrowed the books for a few days; he borrowed the books for a few days only
d the amenity of our streets is recommended to your care; please keep our streets tidy

3 In a brief sentence indicate the use of:

sub judice; ex officio; sine die; persona non grata

4 Write a letter to a firm advising them that goods ordered by you have not arrived to date; urge them to give immediate attention to your order. Also, write their reply.

5 Your employer has become Secretary and Treasurer to a small professional association which has just been formed. He asks you to write the following letters for his signature:

a to a local hotel for the use of a room for the inaugural meeting; a meal will be required
b to the firm's printers, explaining the situation, and asking for samples and quotations for the supply of notepaper and envelopes

Invent a name for the association.

6 Punctuate the following:

robertson chairman and managing director always brought his huge black labrador prince to the office where it would sit with its head between its paws for hours on end there was never much movement from robertson whose secretary joan maintained that after ten years working for him she still could not tell when he was pondering over future company policy or just sound asleep.

Paper four

1 Write the minutes of a Board of Directors' meeting, giving the name of firm, date and time. Include the following:

   a minutes of last meeting to be confirmed
   b presentation of financial statement
   c three other items

2 Use the following words in sentences to show their meaning:

   urban, urbane; treatise, treaties; ordinance, ordnance; hoard, horde

3 Write your letter of application to the following advertisement:

   Manufacturing company in Jurong requires Receptionist/Typist. Must be Singapore citizen aged between 18 and 22 years. Fluent English essential, also some knowledge of Malay and Chinese dialects. Knowledge of operating a PABX switchboard an advantage. Pleasant personality. Apply with full particulars, telephone number, if any, and passport-size photograph (non-returnable) to Personnel Manager, Weldmesh PTE Ltd, Jurong Town, Singapore 22.

4 You work for B Stock & Co Ltd, 1–9 Maple Road, Cartown, Carshire W14 7TS, and a sum of £1500 is 9 months overdue from one of your customers. This money is owed for the printing of catalogues for Crash Mail Order Co, Crash House, Marsh Road, Foden, Rickhamshire, E11 6BA. The long delay is unusual, since Crash Mail Order Co normally pay within 3 months of being invoiced.

   Write a letter, using 150–200 words, to the Chief Accountant of Crash Mail Order Co on behalf of your firm. As you wish to retain the custom of Crash Mail Order Co, your letter should be a reminder rather than a letter of demand. Lay out your letter correctly.

   London Chamber of Commerce exam. paper: Intermediate Stage

5 A customer has written complaining of incivility on the part of a member of the sales staff of your firm. This customer is well-known for his overbearing manner. Write a tactful letter of reply to him.

6 Give antonyms for these words:

   concave; eminent; adversity; trivial; sadness; relapse

Paper five

Summarise the correspondence that follows using not more than 120 words. Show also the list you made before writing the summary of the most important points in each letter.

Mr Thomas Johnson, Chartered Accountant, 8 Pool Road, Blackpool FY3 7SG to Messrs Wilson & Sons, Merchants, 34 Liver House, Liverpool L69 4AN

8 February 19..

With reference to my letter of 25 January I have been informed that your customers Messrs Jameson & Co have announced their insolvency.

Nothing is known at the moment about their assets and liabilities, although I have reason to believe that the position is not very favourable. As soon as I have definite and reliable information I shall write to you again.

If you wish me to represent you in this matter I shall be obliged if you will send me a statement of your account and instructions to act on your behalf.

Messrs Wilson & Sons to Mr Thomas Johnson

10 February 19..

We are surprised to learn from your letter of 8 February that Messrs Jameson & Co have declared their insolvency. Our interest in their business amounts, unfortunately, to £1050.

We enclose a statement of our account, and we shall be glad if you will kindly act for us in this matter.

Enc

Mr Thomas Johnson to Messrs Wilson & Sons

4 March 19..

I have received your letter of 10
February enclosing a statement of your
account with Messrs Jameson & Co and
authorising me to act on your behalf.

At a meeting of the creditors held on
2 March it was agreed to accept an agreement to pay 70p in the £. It was fully
explained at the meeting that if the
estate were declared bankrupt, no more
than 52½p in the £ would be realised,
and that no fault could be attached to
Messrs Jameson & Co.

Although the amount of your loss is large,
I think that in the circumstances you will
agree that the best course has been taken.

Payment will be made in three dividends of
equal amounts, on 1 July, 1 September and
1 November of this year, and the three
solvent guarantors are security for the
carrying out of the arrangements.

If you wish, I shall be pleased to collect
your dividends as they become due, and to
hold them awaiting your instructions.

Messrs Wilson & Sons to Mr Thomas Johnson

7 March 19..

We have received your letter of 4 March
informing us that Messrs Jameson & Co have
agreed to pay 70p in the £. We agree
to this arrangement.

As suggested we shall be obliged if you
will collect our dividends when due and
hold them pending further instructions
from us.

Paper six

1 Carefully read the following passage, which contains about 400 words. Then, *using your own words as far as possible*, write a summary of it in not more than 120 words. Finally, supply an appropriate title for your summary.

There are still many businesses in which advertising plays a very minor role, and such advertising as is done is confined to trade publications. Many firms producing for industrial markets are in this position, though it is significant that some of the most important and far-seeing organisations take space in the national press in the form of 'prestige' or 'institutional' advertising as part of their public relations campaigns. A firm of steel tube manufacturers, by means of a series of humorous advertisements on London underground trains, even made themselves a household word far beyond the industrial buyers they would generally expect to reach.

Nevertheless, the great bulk of advertising and sales promotion expenditure, now running at well over £500 million a year, is spent by producers on consumer markets. Of all forms of marketing expenditure, advertising is the largest single item, and mistakes can be, and frequently are, costly. They are, moreover, easy to make, for of all skills advertising seems to be most subject to chance in its results. Many marketing and advertising managers, when asked to what extent their advertising has contributed to the success or otherwise of a marketing campaign, will freely admit that they cannot say. There are too many imponderables, just as there are imponderables in the creative arts, with which advertising has something in common, which makes it impossible to forecast a best seller or the likely acceptability of a picture or a piece of music.

The possibilities of investigation into the complex of human relations in which advertising seeks to make its impact are for this reason obviously limited, and even when investigation takes place, in the nature of things it can do so only after the money has been spent. Thus the knowledge gained is the knowledge of hindsight, applicable only to the campaign which is over and only dubiously to the campaign which is to come under new conditions. Results in terms of sales can never be obtained except in the case of 'keyed' advertisements—that is, advertisements which carry a coupon to be filled in by the reader or which invite some other action which can be checked back afterwards. The keyed advertisement, indeed, is almost as much an instrument of research in itself as a method of selling, for by its means mailing lists can be compiled and the pulling power both of the medium and of the advertisement can be accurately assessed.

London Chamber of Commerce exam. paper: Intermediate Stage

2 Make clear the meaning of the following in any way you choose:

hackneyed expression   ingratiating behaviour
fait accompli   to work to rule
tacit agreement   cursory glance

3 The office manager of the firm for which you work—S W Gilbert & Co Ltd, High Street, Postford, Wessex W12 8ZY—has asked you to write a letter of complaint to T White & Co Ltd, East Road, Banner Park, London E21 4TU. For the fifth time this year deliveries of components for the radios which Gilbert & Co make have been much later in arriving than White & Co had promised. This has held up radio production and caused complaints from customers. Explain this in your letter, adding any other relevant points you think should be made. Inform T White & Co Ltd that, if this happens again, your firm may be forced to go elsewhere for supplies. Your letter should be between 150 and 200 words.

London Chamber of Commerce exam. paper: Intermediate Stage

4 The managers of the branches of your firm are coming to Head Office for a conference. They are to stay for three days at the same hotel; a room will be required for conference purposes during the time of their visit. Write a letter of inquiry to the hotel giving full details of the requirements.

5 You have been sent by the Managing Director of your firm to make preliminary inquiries regarding a possible site for a factory in north-east Scotland. Write the report, supplying names and details.

6 What, in your view, are the essential differences between a secretary and a shorthand typist? Write your answer in 4 paragraphs not exceeding 250 words.

Abbreviations: commercial and general

These lists by no means represent a comprehensive coverage of general business terms; they do, however, include the more common abbreviations.

@	at
A1	first class (at Lloyds)
a/c	account
acc	acceptance or accepted
AD	anno Domini; in the year of our Lord
ad lib	at your pleasure; as much as you like
ad val	ad valorem; according to the value
adv	advice
advt	advertisement
agt	agent
am	ante meridiem; before noon
amt	amount
anon	anonymous
ans	answer
app	appendix
appro	approval
approx	approximate
arr	arrival
assoc	association
asst	assistant
av	average
bal	balance
BC	before Christ
B/D	bank draft
b/e	bill of exchange
b/f	brought forward
bk	book; bank
Bros	brothers

BR	British Rail
BRS	British Rail Services
C	centigrade (thermometer scale); cent; a hundred
c & f	cost and freight
caps	capitals
cc	copies
cert	certificate
cf	compare
ch; chap	chapter
chq	cheque
cif	cost, insurance, and freight
cif & c	cost, insurance, freight, and commission
cm	centimetre
C/N	credit note
Co	Company; county
c/o	care of; carried over
COD	cash on delivery; Concise Oxford Dictionary
col	column
cr	credit
cum div	with dividend
d/d	days after date
deg	degree
dep	depart
dept	department
dis	discount
ditto; do	the same
div	dividend, division
D/N	debit note
D/O	delivery order
doz	dozen
dr	debtor
DV	Deo volente; God willing
ee	errors excepted
e & oe	errors and omissions excepted
eg	exempli gratia; for example
enc; encl	enclosure
etc	et cetera; and the rest
et seq	et sequentia; and the following
ex	from out of; without
ex div	without dividend

F; Fahr	Fahrenheit (thermometer scale)
fig	figure
fob	free on board
fwd	forward
g	gram
govt	government
gr	gross
gr wt	gross weight
hp	horsepower
HP	hire purchase
HQ	headquarters
ib; ibid	ibidem; in the same place
id	idem; the same
ie	id est; that is
in trans	in transitu; on the way
Inc	Incorporated
ins	insurance
int	interest
inv	invoice
IOU	I owe you
ital	italics
JP	Justice of the Peace
jr	junior
£	libra; a pound (sterling)
l; lit	litre
l/c	letter of credit
m	metre
max	maximum
mem; memo	memorandum
mg	milligram
min	minimum; minute
mm	millimetre
MP	Member of Parliament
mph	miles per hour
ms	manuscript
mth	month

NB	nota bene; take careful note
no	number
non seq	non sequitur; it does not follow
o/a	on account
oct (8vo)	octavo
o/d	on demand
O/D	overdraft
OHMS	On Her Majesty's Service
o/s	outstanding; out of stock
p; pp	page; pages
PA	Personal Assistant; Power of Attorney
PC	police constable
pc	postcard
pcl	parcel
pd	paid
per pro; pp	per procurationem; on behalf of
pkg	package
pkt	packet
pl	plural
pm	post meridiem; after noon
PM	Prime Minister
pro	on behalf of
pro tem	pro tempore; for the time being
PS	post scriptum; postscript, added after the signature to a letter
PPS	post post scriptum; a second postscript
PTO	please turn over
qto (4to)	quarto
qv	quod vide; which see; to which you should refer
rd	road
re	in regard to; relating to
recd	received
ref	referred; reference
regd	registered
retd	returned
rly	railway
RSVP	répondez s'il vous plaît; reply, if you please

$	dollar(s)
sae	stamped addressed envelope
sec	second
secy	secretary
senr	senior
sgd	signed
S/O	standing order
soc	society
sq	square
SS	steamship
St	saint; street
std	standard
stg	sterling
t	tonne (=1000 kg)
temp	tempore; in the period of
u/w	underwritten
v	versus; against
via	by way of
VIP	very important person
viz	videlicet; namely
vol	volume
wk	week
wt	weight
yr	year

Index